RHYMING WORDS
KINDERGARTEN

1 SHEETS

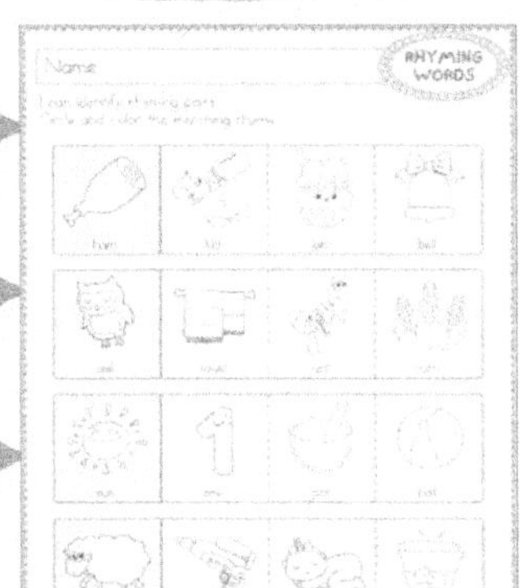

FUN PHONICS AWARENESS
LEARNING TO READ

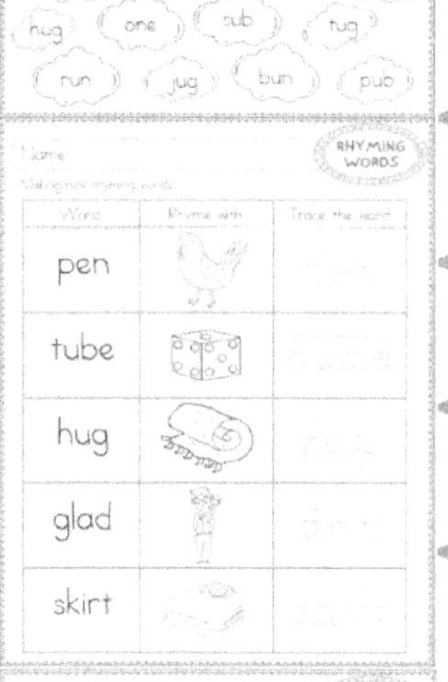

Name:

I can identify rhyming pairs.
Circle and color the matching rhyme.

RHYMING WORDS

I can identify rhyming pairs.
Circle and color the matching rhyme.

Name:

I can identify rhyming pairs.
Circle and color the matching rhyme.

Name:

I can identify rhyming pairs.
Circle and color the matching rhyme.

Name:

I can identify rhyming pairs.
Circle and color the matching rhyme.

Name:

I can identify rhyming pairs.
Circle and color the matching rhyme.

Name:

Read the word and color one that rhymes with the picture.

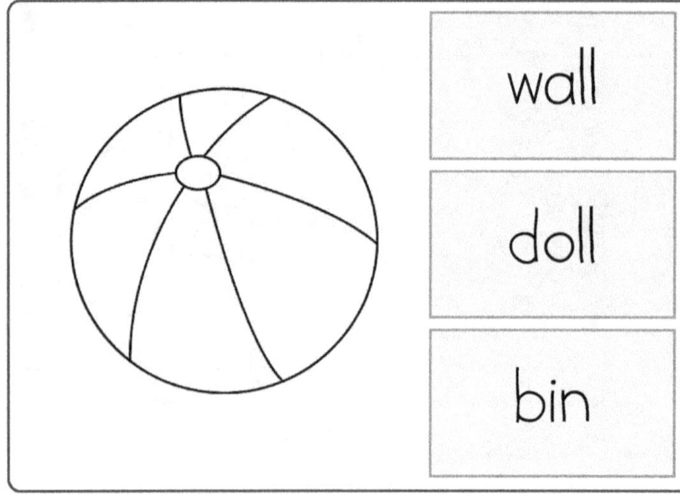

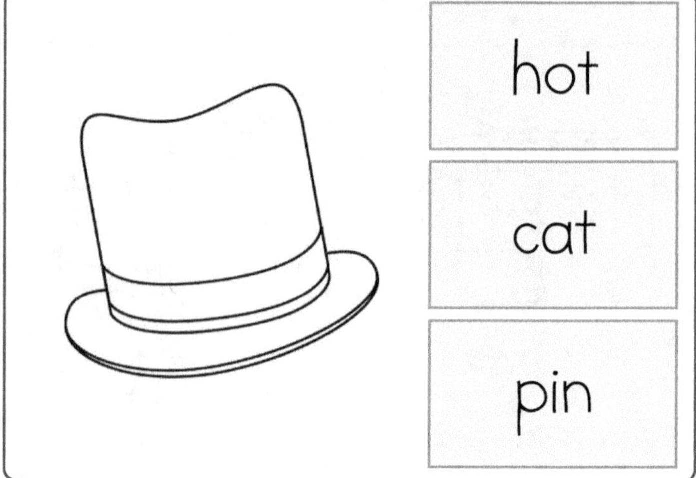

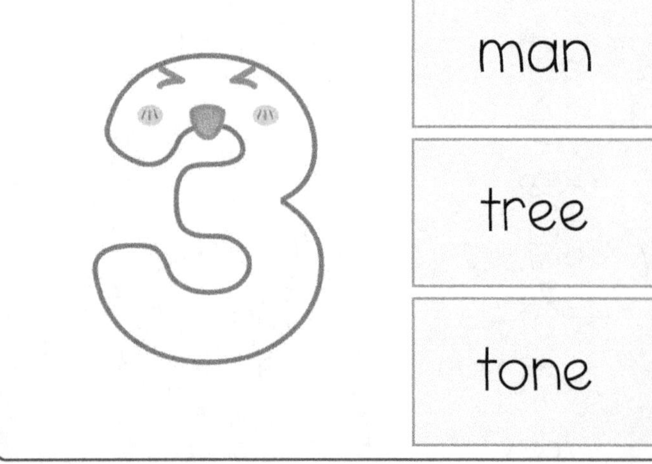

Name:

Read the word and color one that rhymes with the picture.

aunt

pat

ball

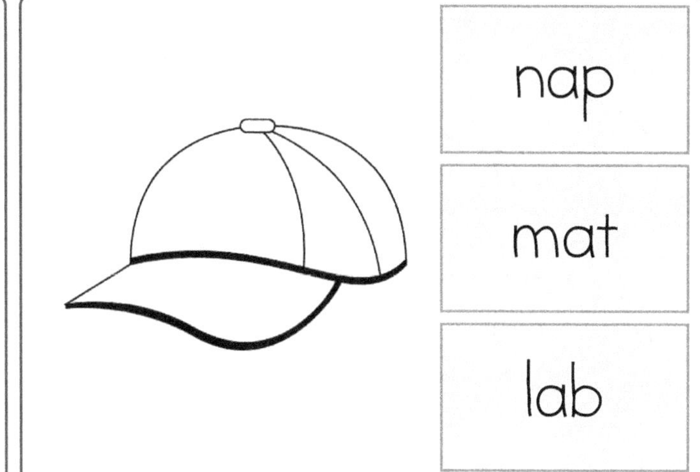

nap

mat

lab

nine

jam

part

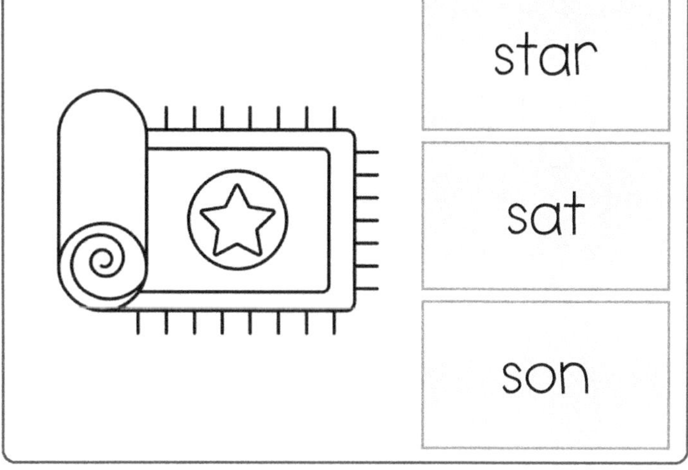

star

sat

son

got

gate

get

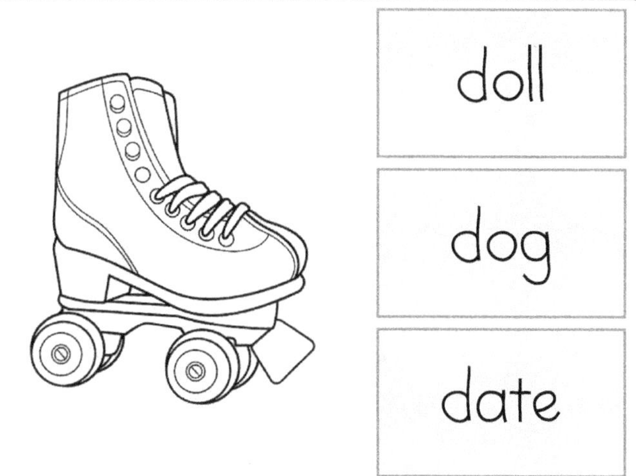

doll

dog

date

Name:

Read the word and color one that rhymes with the picture.

hut

head

home

sad

sun

see

art

my

and

king

keep

kind

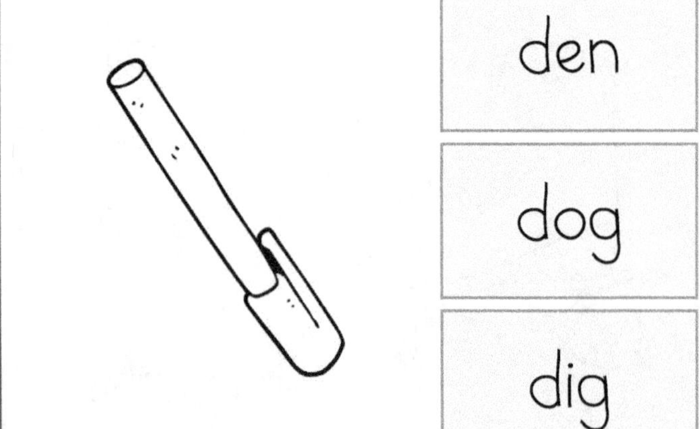

den

dog

dig

sock

sand

sick

Name: ___________________

Read the word and color one that rhymes with the picture.

mud

men

man

luck

long

land

have

wish

went

then

than

three

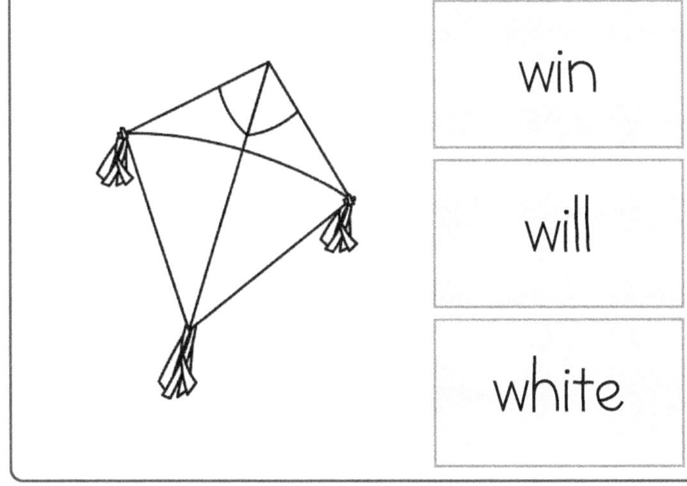

win

will

white

note

nine

none

Name:

Read the word and color one that rhymes with the picture.

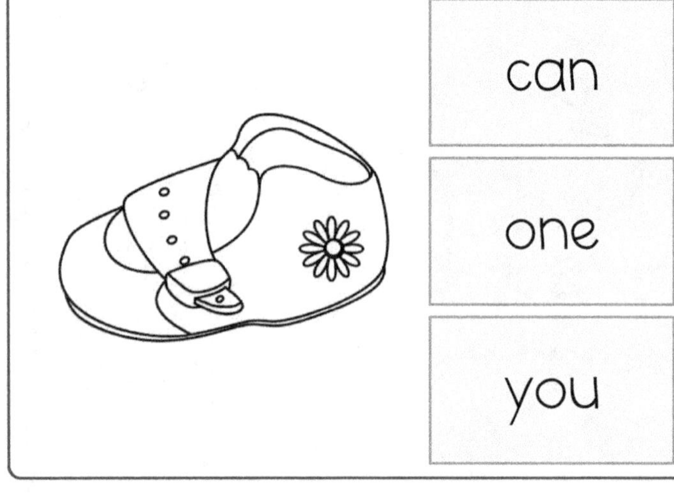

RHYMING WORDS

Name:

Read the word and color one that rhymes with the picture.

for

big

bog

lag

jam

man

deep

done

den

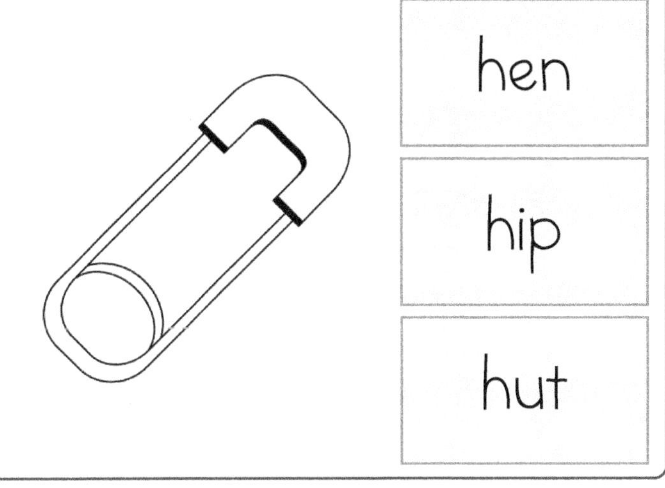

hen

hip

hut

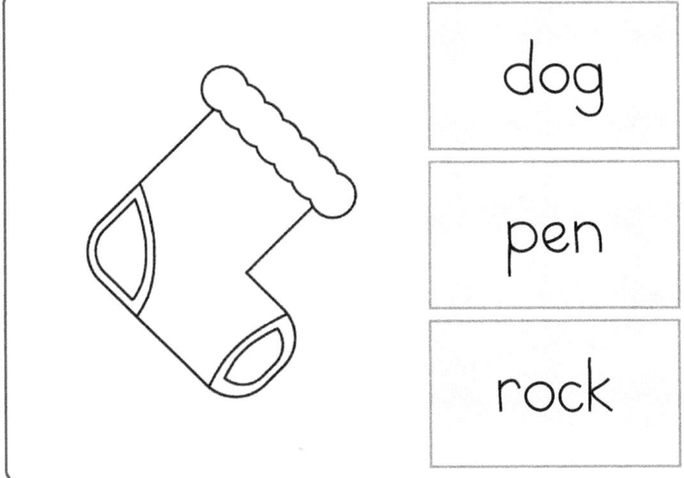

dog

pen

rock

who

gut

bat

Name: _______________

Read the word and color one that rhymes with the picture.

sun
dug
big

four
three
two

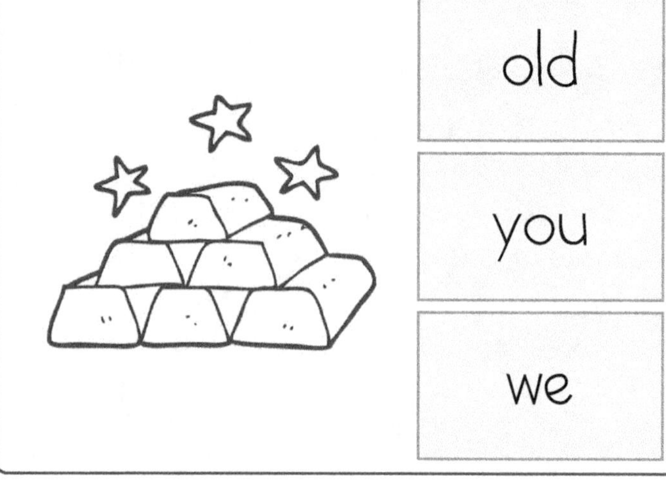

old
you
we

green
blue
shoe

make
play
cold

hook
they
from

Name:

Read the word and color one that rhymes with the picture.

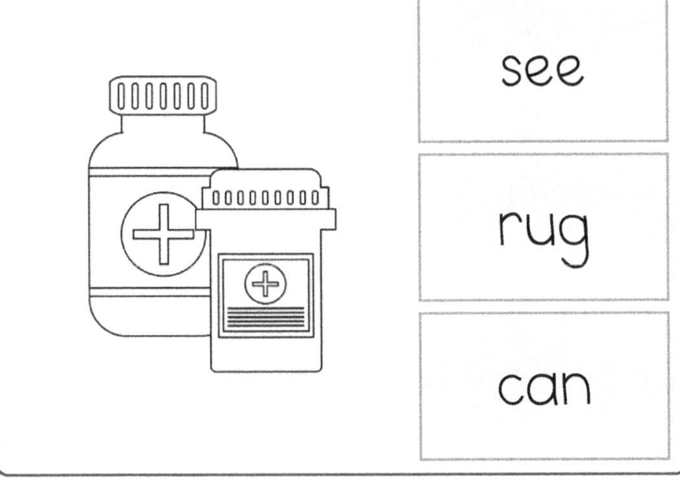

see

rug

can

moon

black

make

door

down

they

sun

for

like

him

has

hug

her

rub

all

Name:

Read the word and color one that rhymes with the picture.

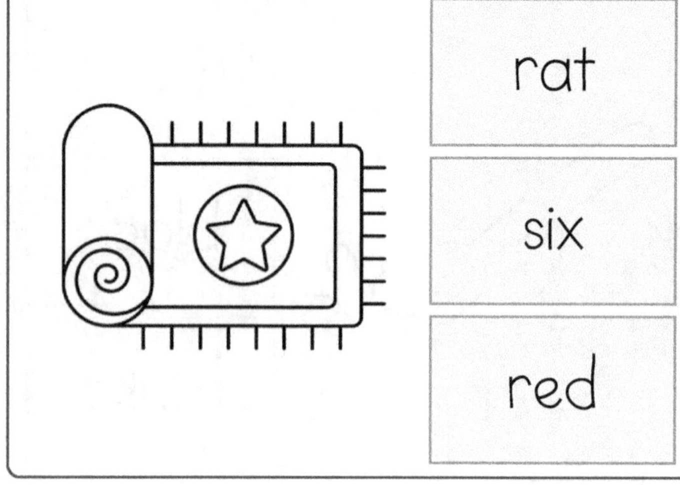

rat

six

red

too

run

my

nine

jug

good

drag

five

pink

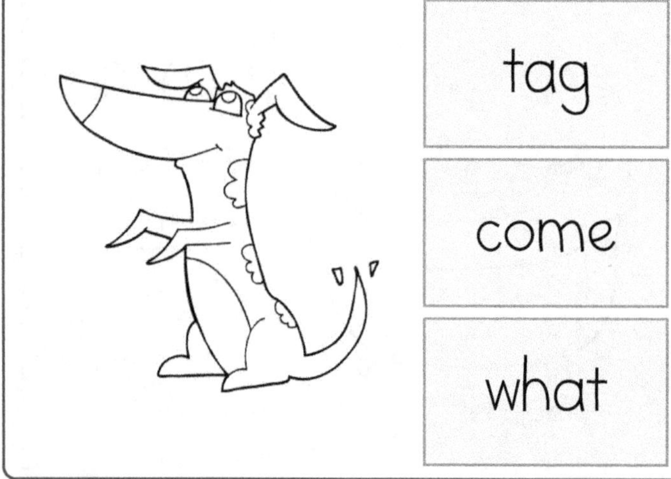

tag

come

what

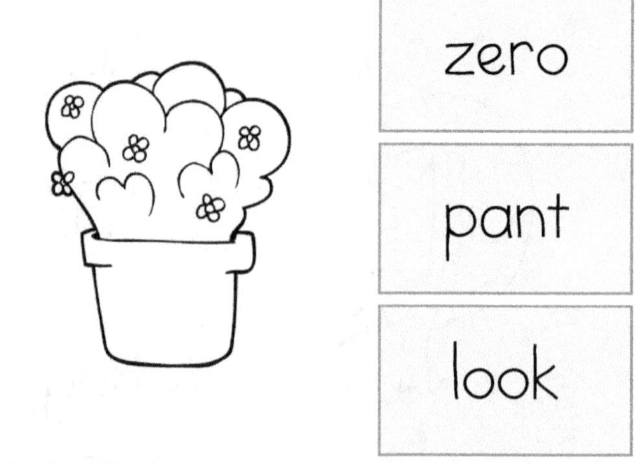

zero

pant

look

Name:

Read the word and color one that rhymes with the picture.

little

three

sheep

said

block

heart

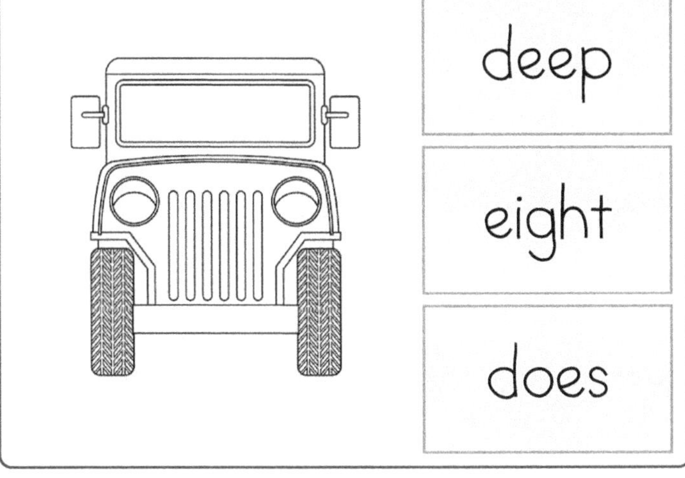

deep

eight

does

old

one

do

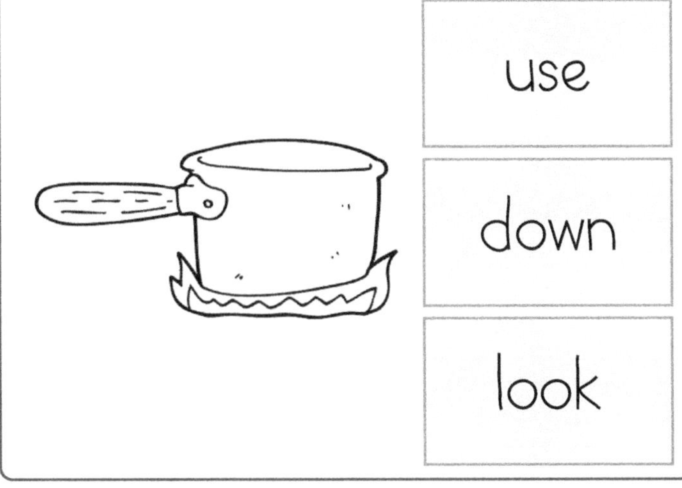

use

down

look

hut

not

for

RHYMING WORDS

Trace the word that rhymes with picture in each row.

Name:

Trace the word that rhymes with picture in each row.

(hearts)	hat part
(hat)	cat pot
(rug)	nap hat
(8)	gate cats
(plate with fork)	wait pan

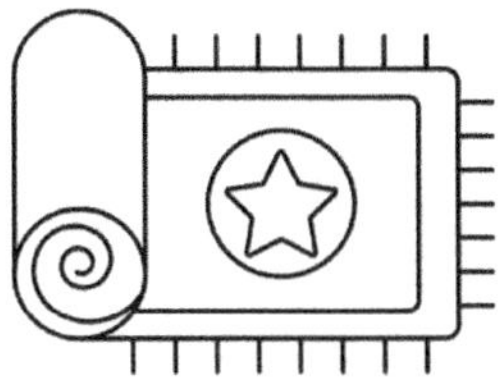

Name:

Trace the word that rhymes with picture in each row.

Name:

Trace the word that rhymes with picture in each row.

Name:

Trace the word that rhymes with picture in each row.

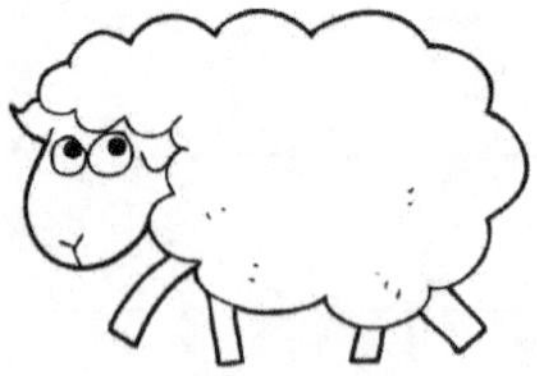

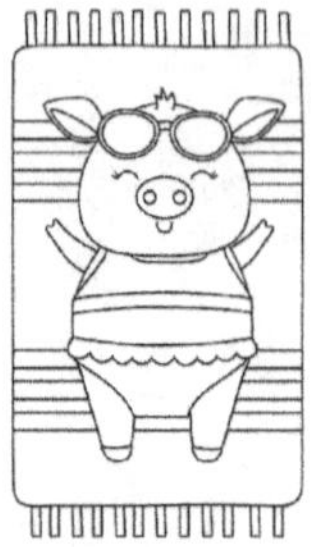

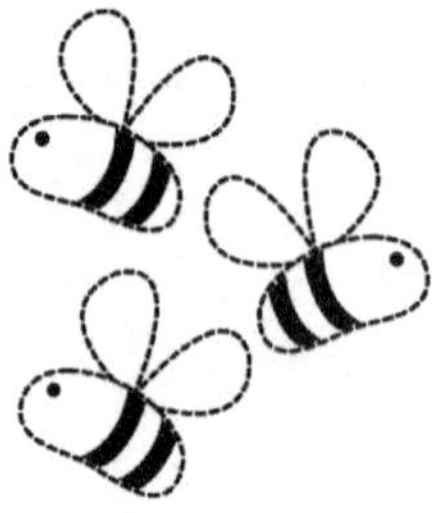

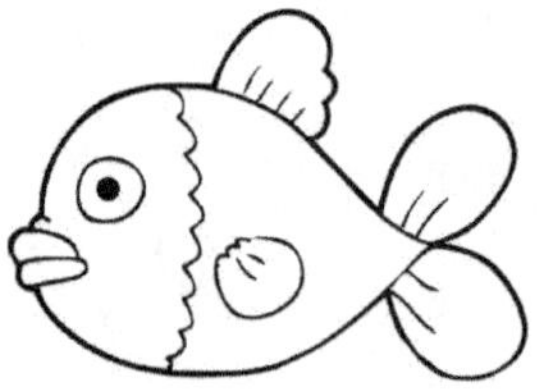

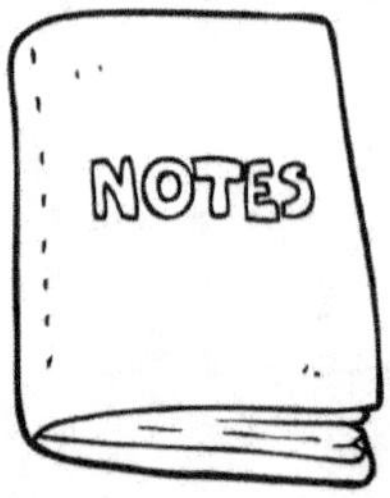

Name:

Trace the word that rhymes with picture in each row.

	duck did
	hog hut
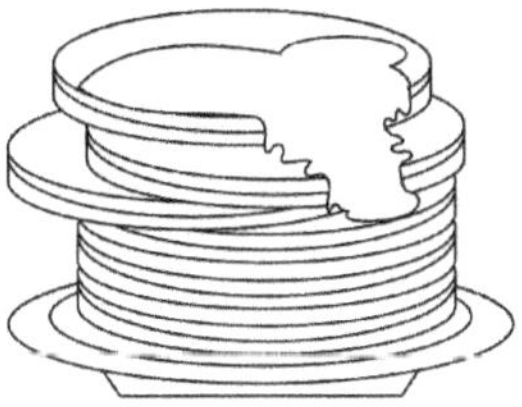	fish fat
	log dig
	can hold

Name:

Trace the word that rhymes with picture in each row.

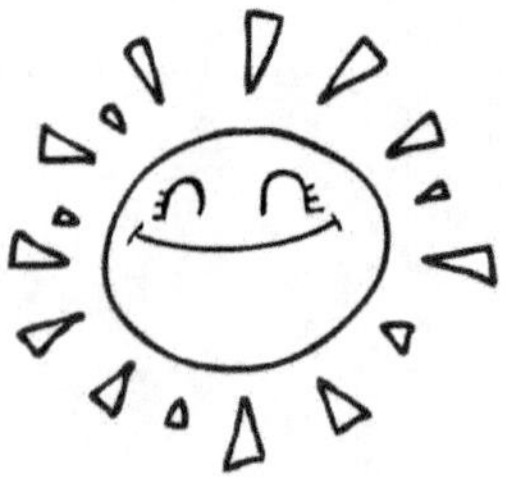

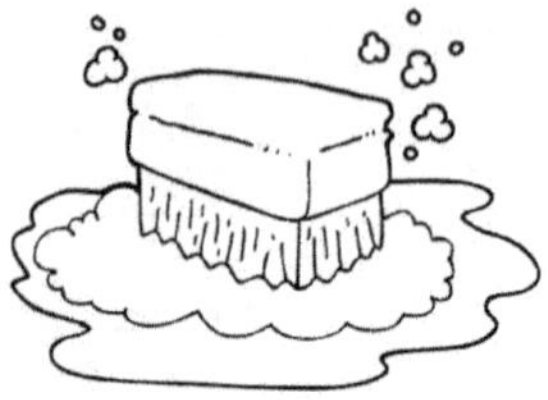

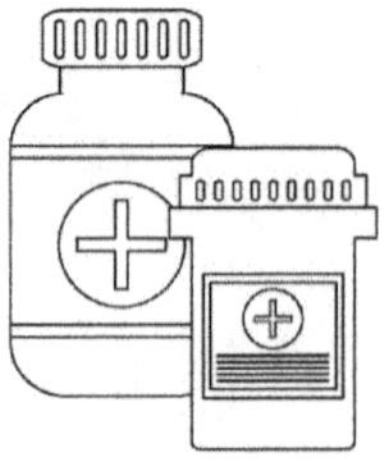

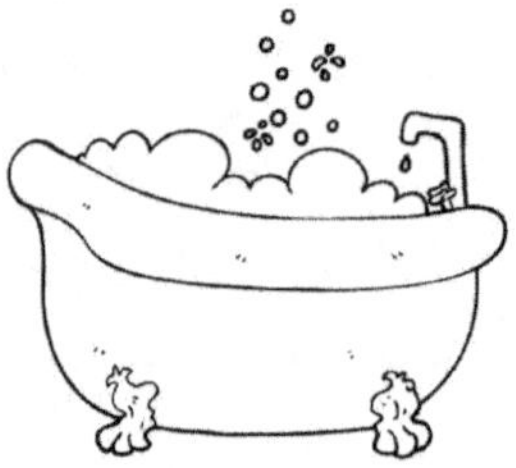

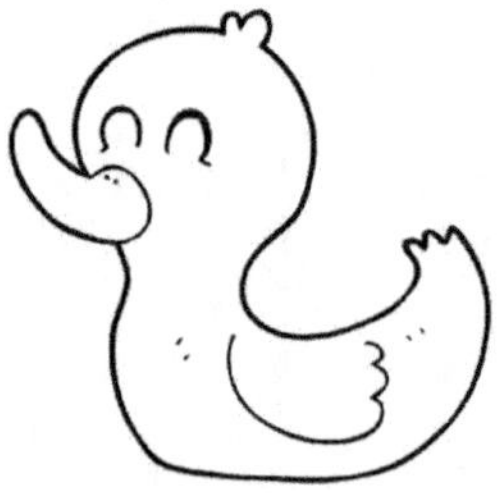

Name:

Trace the word that rhymes with picture in each row.

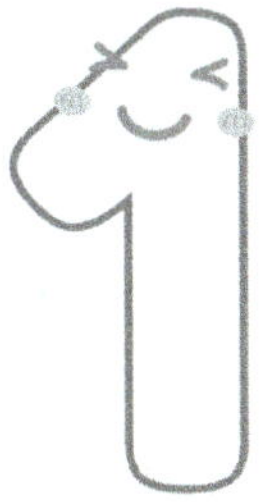 1	sick sun
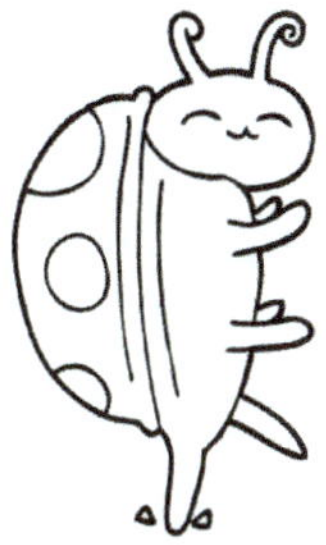	hug hut
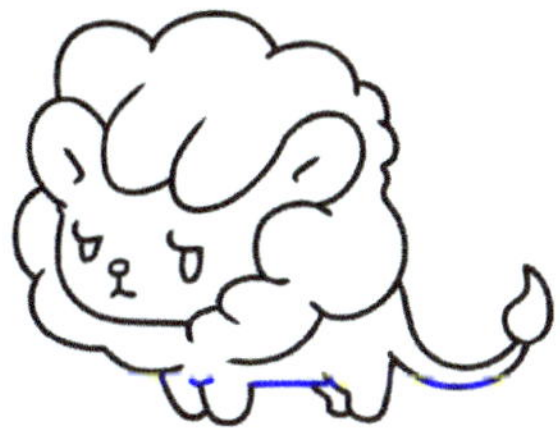	rub fat
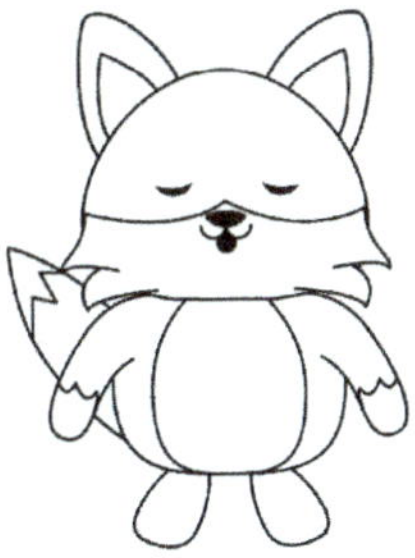	rug box
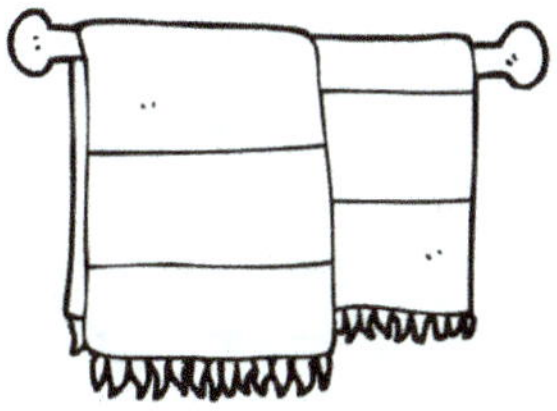	can owl

Name:

Trace the word that rhymes with picture in each row.

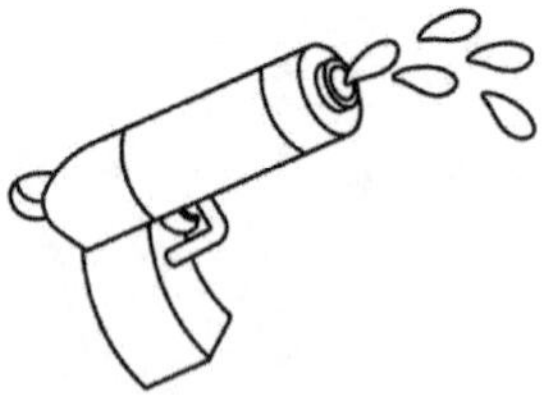

fun   fat

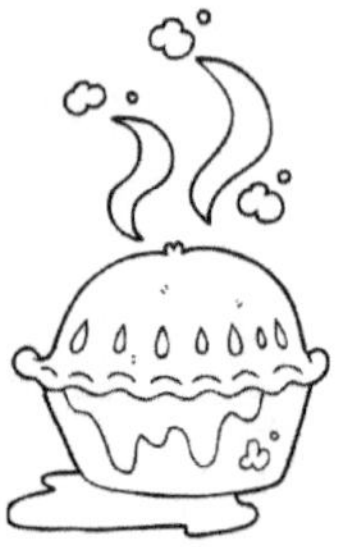

hat   pot

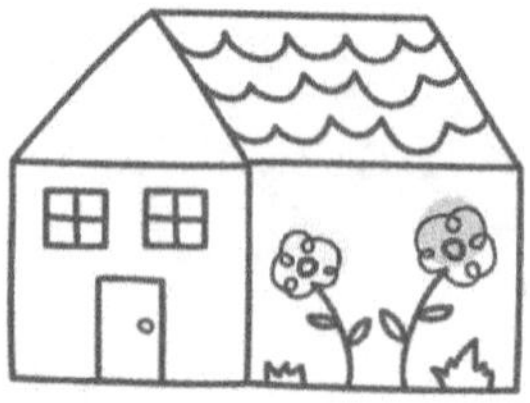

mouse   tub

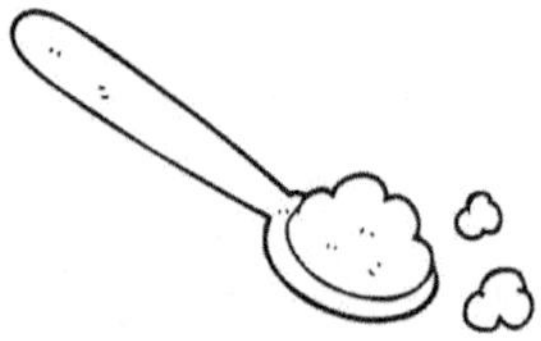

moon   mat

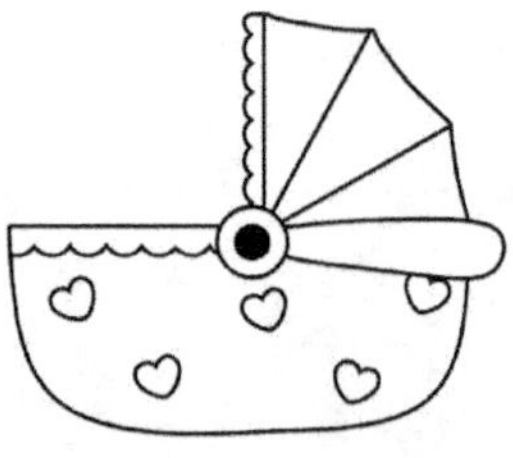

hat   not

Name:

Trace the word that rhymes with picture in each row.

(pot)	dog dot
(book)	look big
(balloon)	moon pin
(mouse)	rug house
(moon)	son spoon

Name:

Color and draw a line to join the rhyming words together.

ant

heart

bag

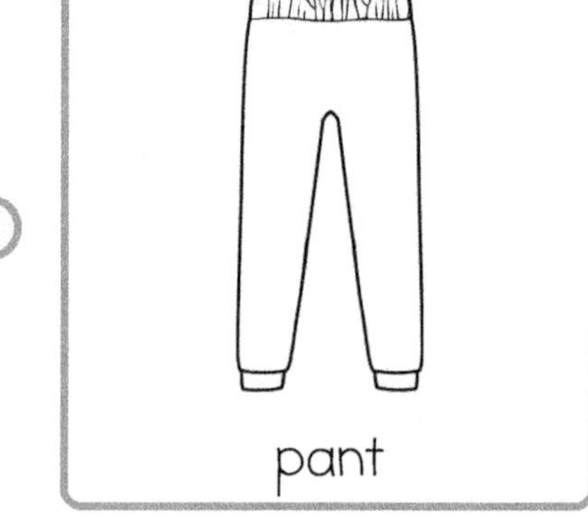

pant

tart

flag

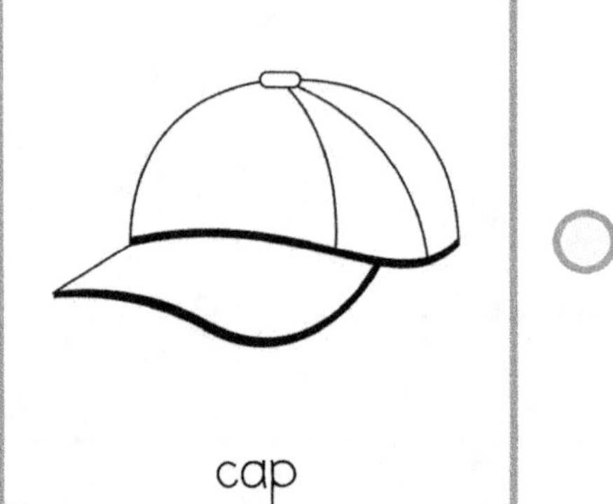

cap

nap

Name:

Color and draw a line to join the rhyming words together.

tag

fall

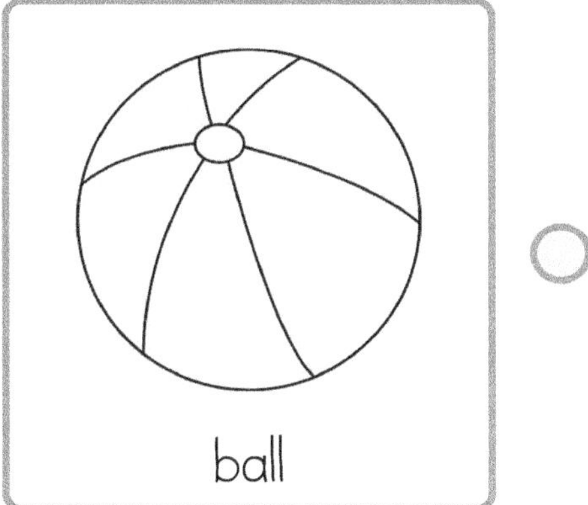

ball

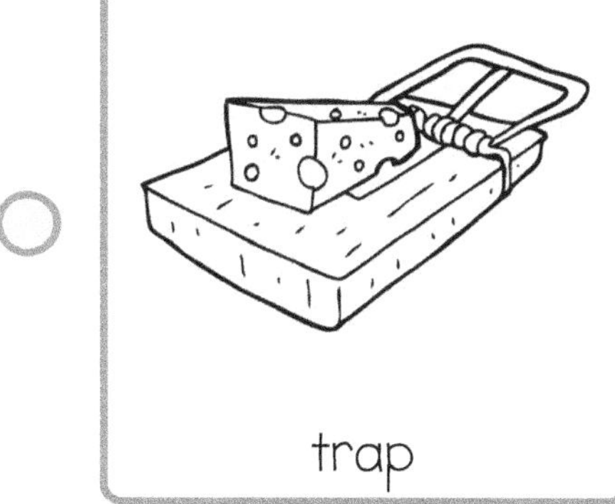

trap

map

dart

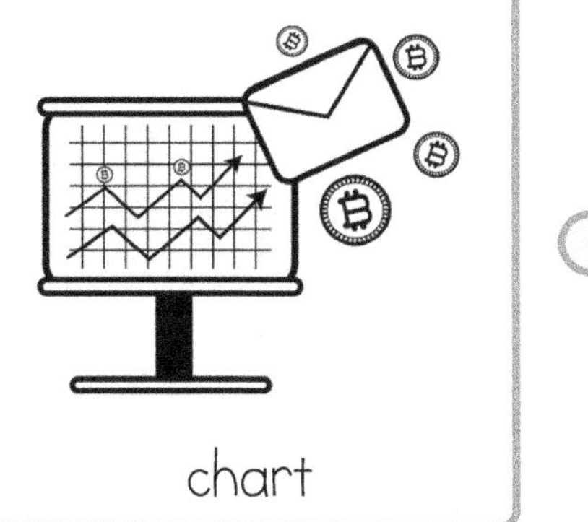

chart

wag

Name:

Color and draw a line to join the rhyming words together.

mall

fat

cat

tall

eight

wed

bread

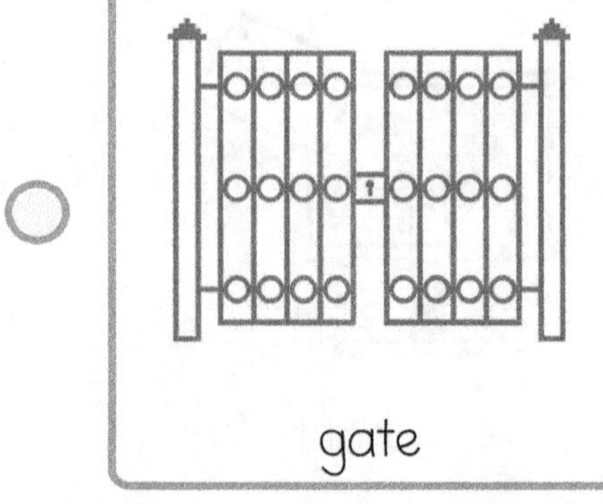

gate

Name:

Color and draw a line to join the rhyming words together.

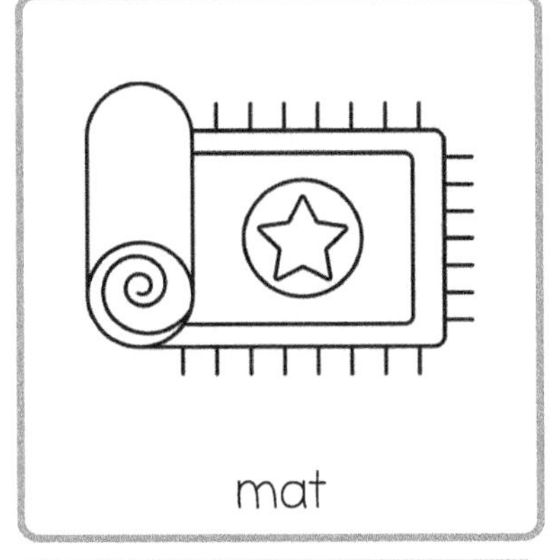

mat

hat

plate

key

bee

skate

jeep

sheep

Name:

Color and draw a line to join the rhyming words together.

three

hen

sweep

sleep

men

kick

chick

tree

Name:

Color and draw a line to join the rhyming words together.

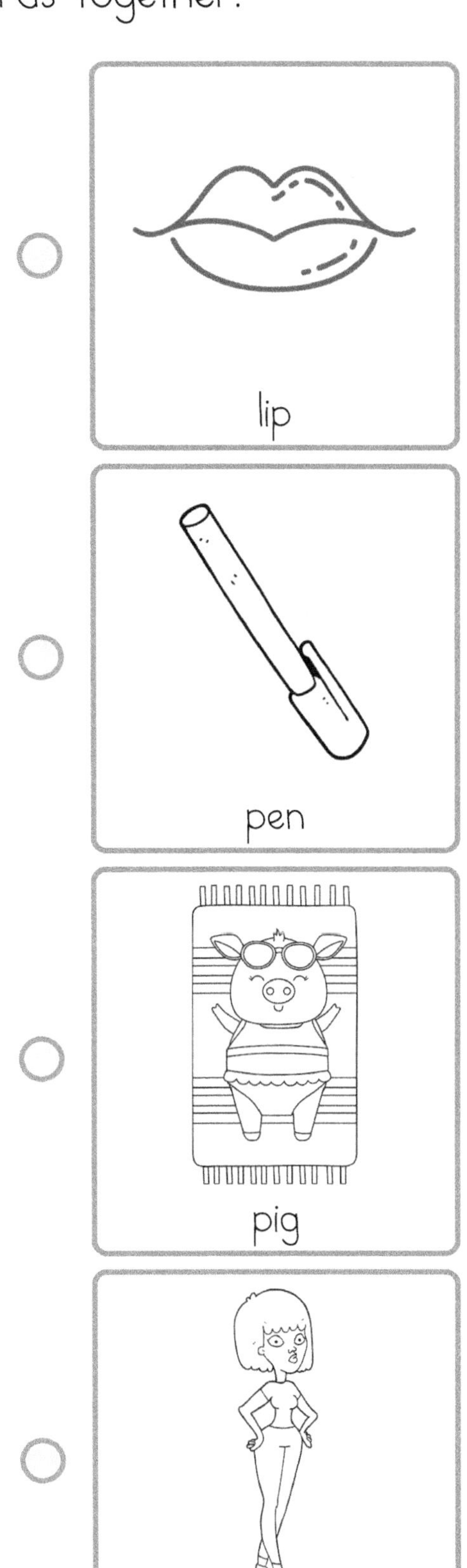

Name:

Color and draw a line to join the rhyming words together.

dish

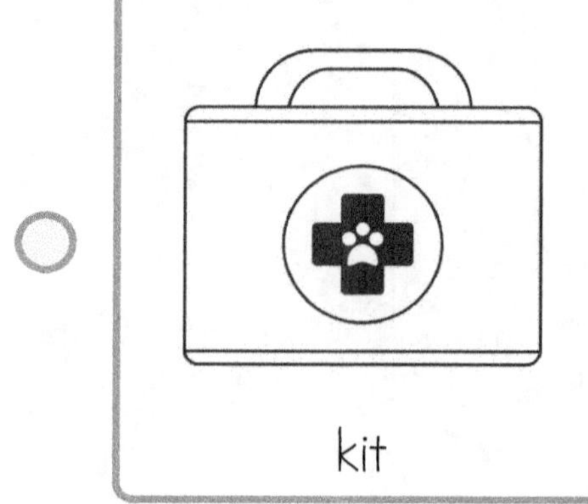

kit

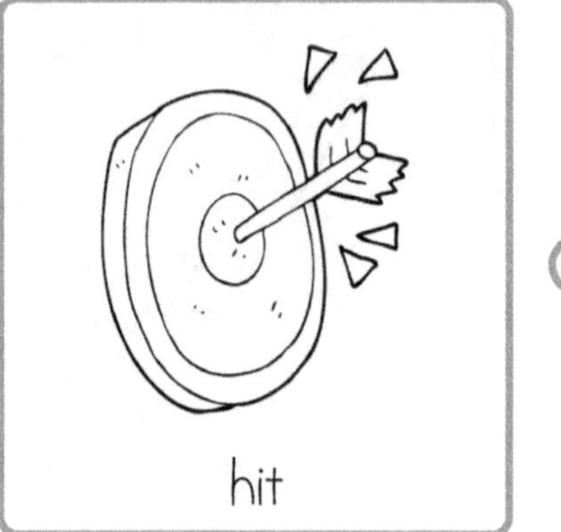

hit

night

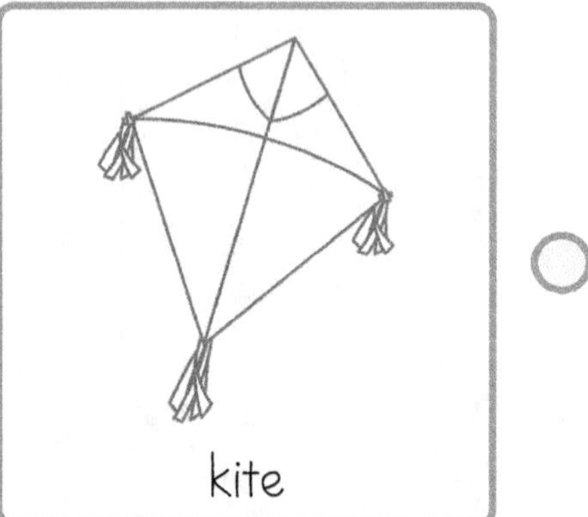

kite

fish

goat

oat

Name:

Color and draw a line to join the rhyming words together.

clock

lock

pig

sit

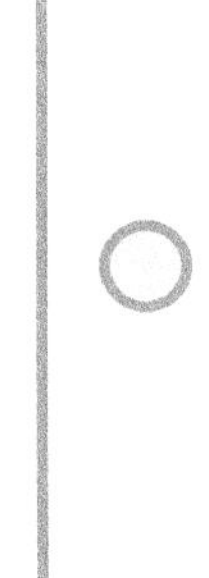

drip

hip

lit

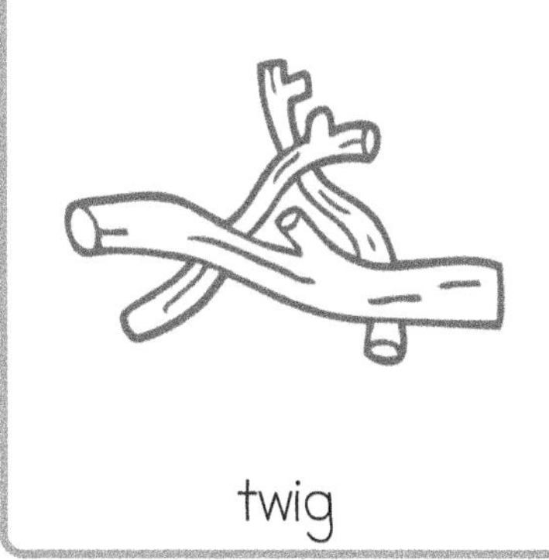

twig

Name:

For each of the below words, find and write 1 rhyming word.

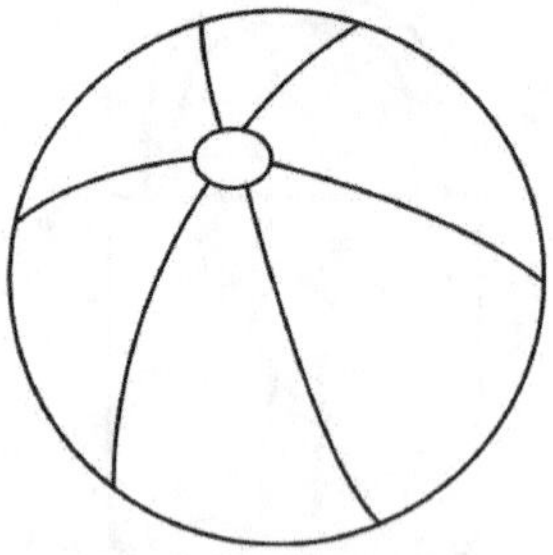

ball

fall

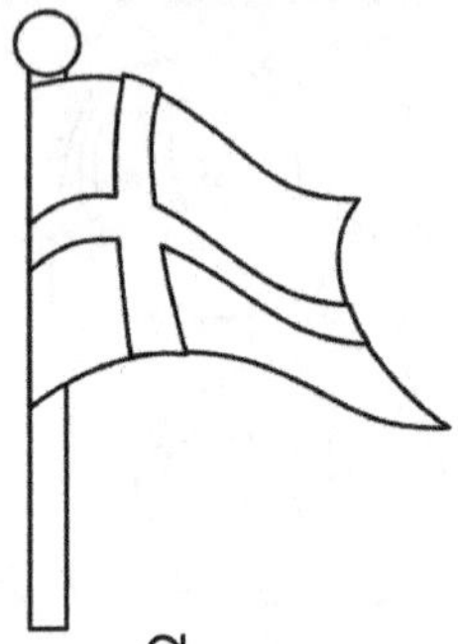

flag

tag

ant

plant

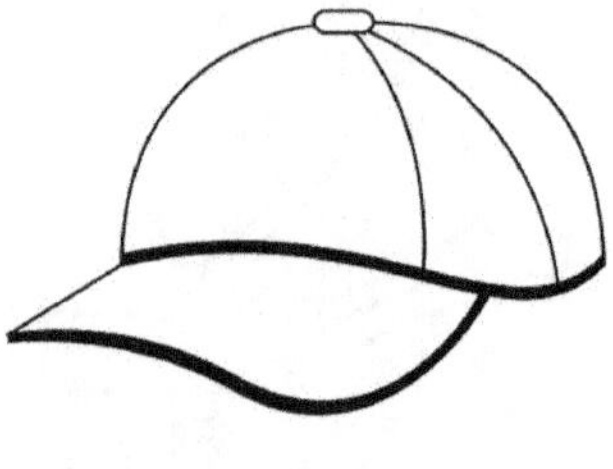

cap

nap

Name:

For each of the below words, find and write 1 rhyming word.

Name: _______________________________

For each of the below words, find and write 1 rhyming word.

Name:

For each of the below words, find and write 1 rhyming word.

jeep

sheep

tree

three

key

bee

skate

plate

Name:

For each of the below words, find and write 1 rhyming word.

Name:

For each of the below words, find and write 1 rhyming word.

Name:

For each of the below words, find and write 1 rhyming word.

Name:

For each of the below words, find and write 1 rhyming word.

two

shoe

dog

frog

old

gold

note

oat

Name:

For each of the below words, find and write 1 rhyming word.

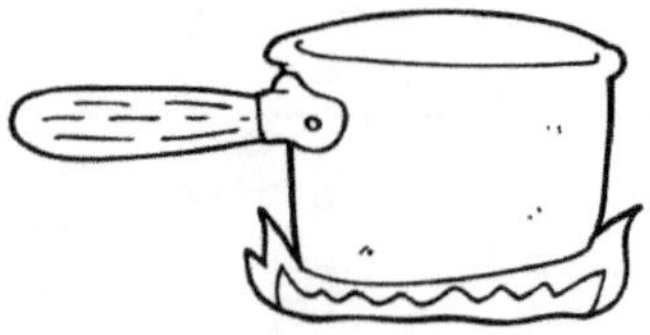

cook

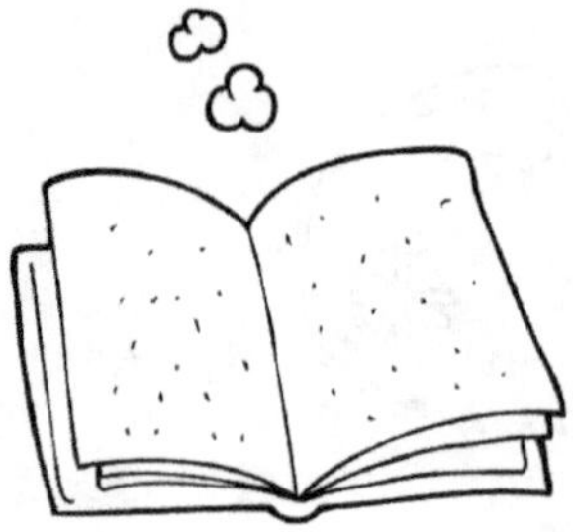

book

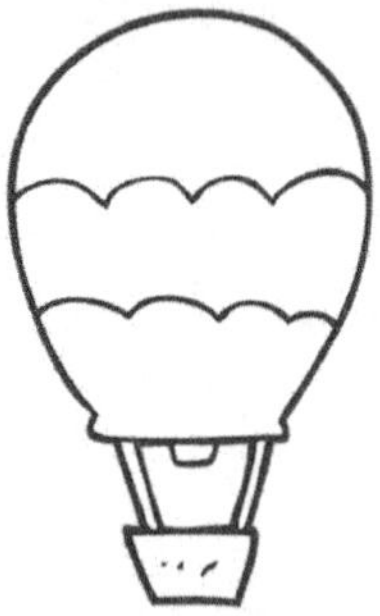

____

balloon

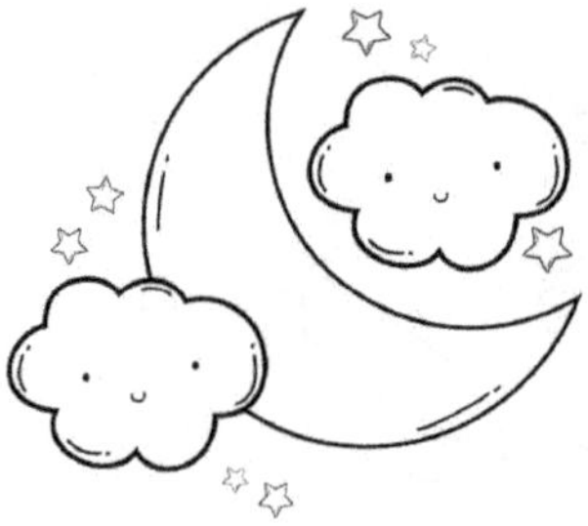

moon

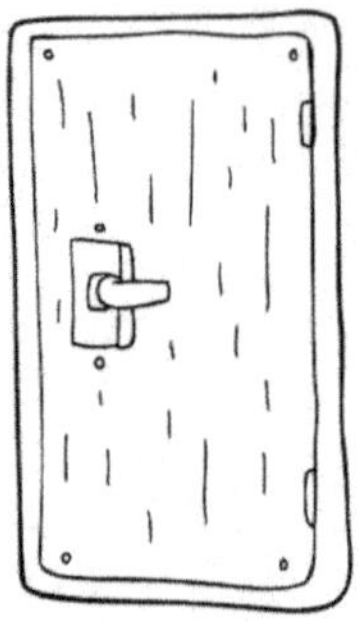

____

door

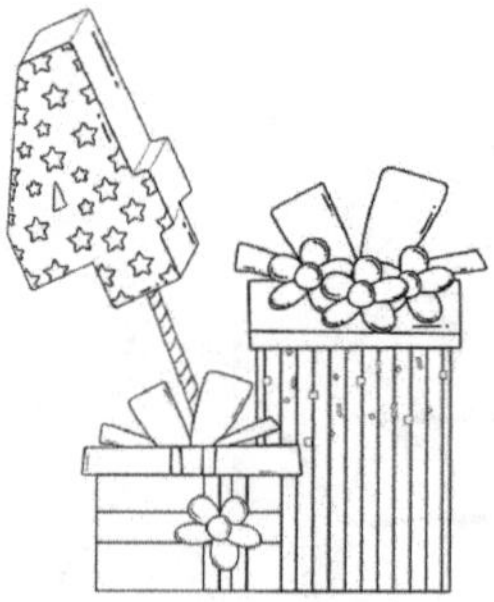

four

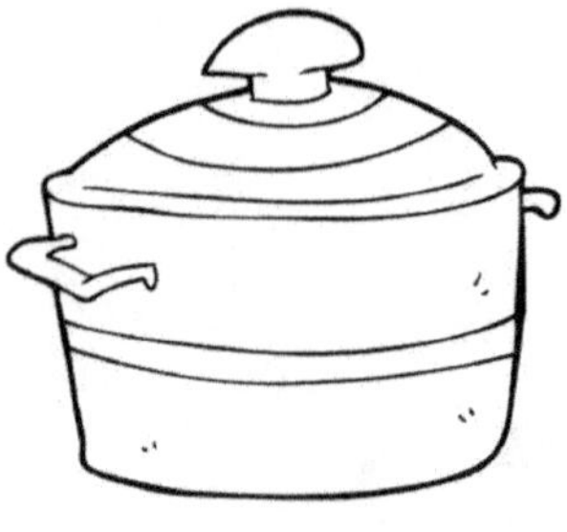

____

pot

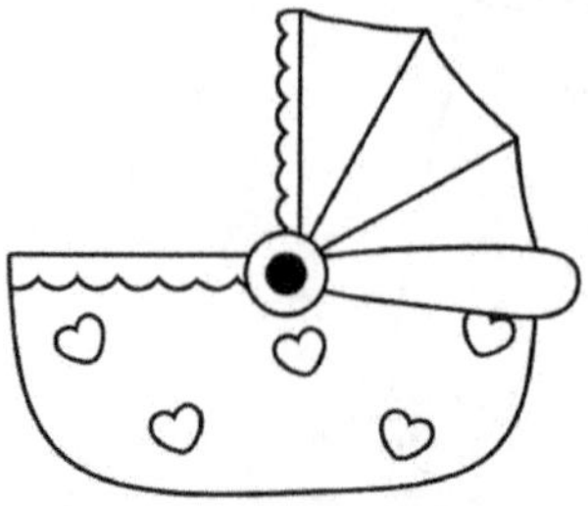

cot

____

Name: _______________

For each of the below words, find and write 1 rhyming word.

Name:

For each of the below words, find and write 1 rhyming word.

Name:

For each of the below words, find and write 1 rhyming word.

Name:

For each of the below words, find and write 1 rhyming word.

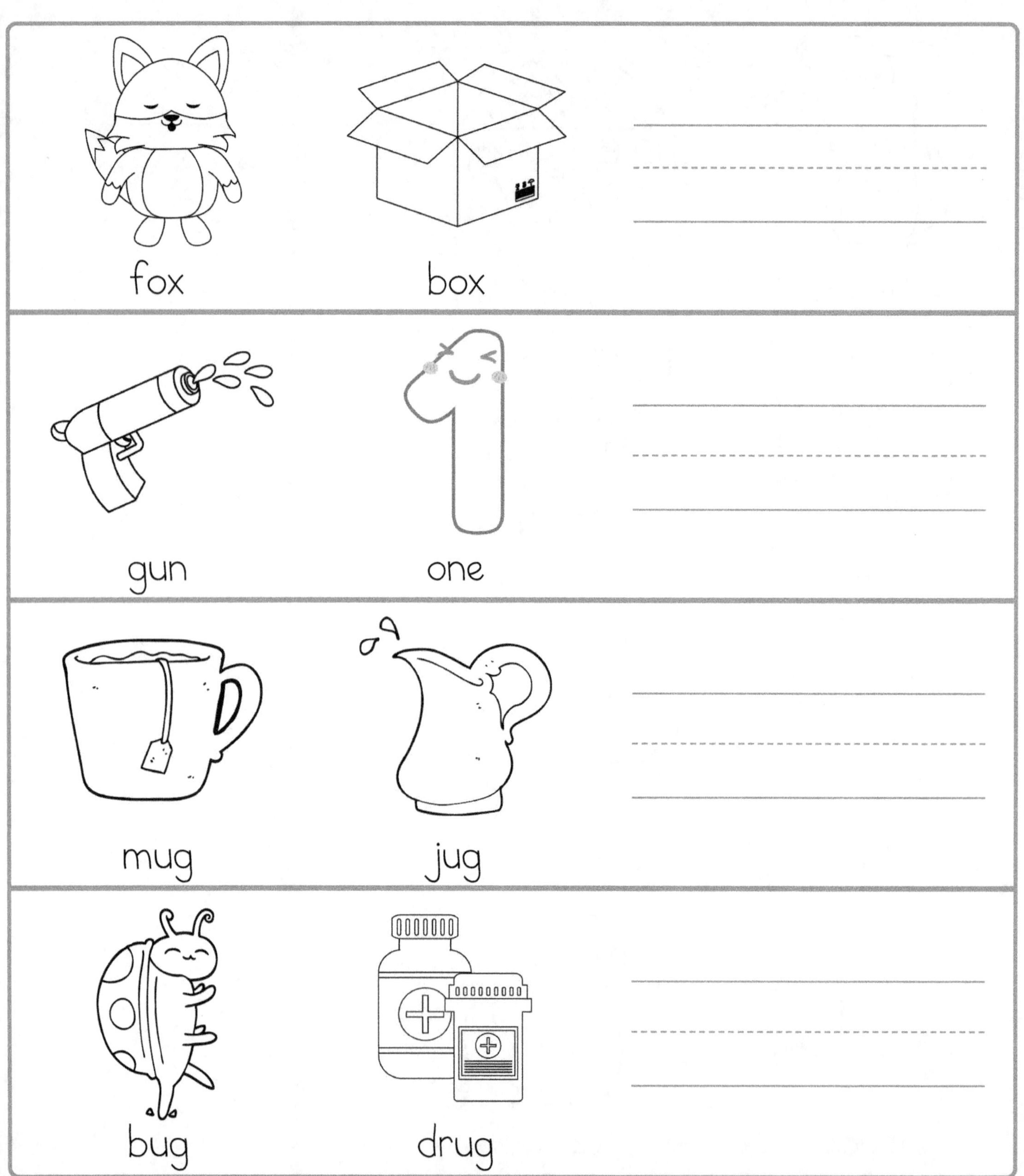

RHYME TIME

Name:

Choose and write the word to the correct section.

ball	hen	tree

RHYME TIME

Choose and write the word to the correct section.

hat	bee	dog

Name:

RHYME TIME

Choose and write the word to the correct section.

bag	nap	pot

RHYME TIME

Name:

Choose and write the word to the correct section.

sun	tub	mug

RHYME TIME

Choose and write the word to the correct section.

♥	🛏	🧰
heart	bed	tree

Name:

RHYME TIME

Choose and write the word to the correct section.

RHYME TIME

Name:

Choose and write the word to the correct section.

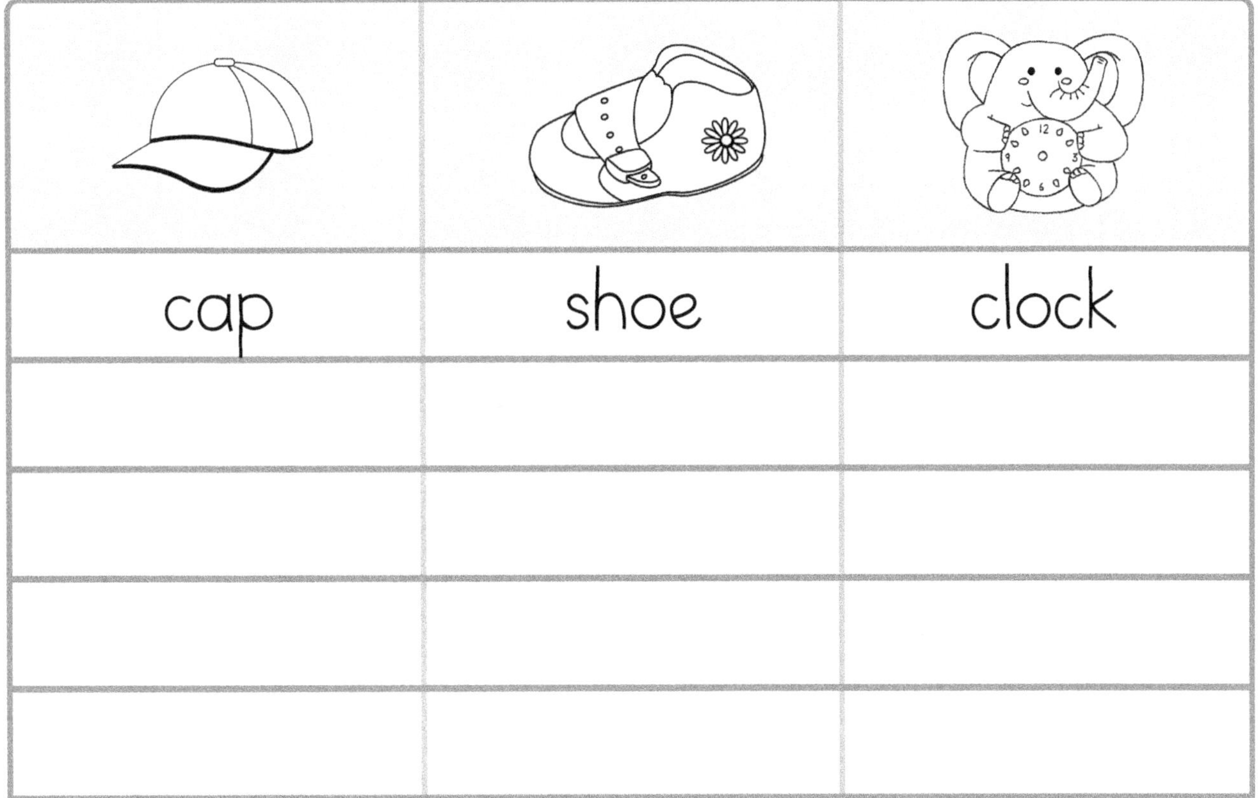

Name:

Say the picture in the middle. Circle the pictures that rhymes with it. Trace the rhyming words below.

ant   pant   plant

Name:

Say the picture in the middle. Circle the pictures that rhymes with it. Trace the rhyming words below.

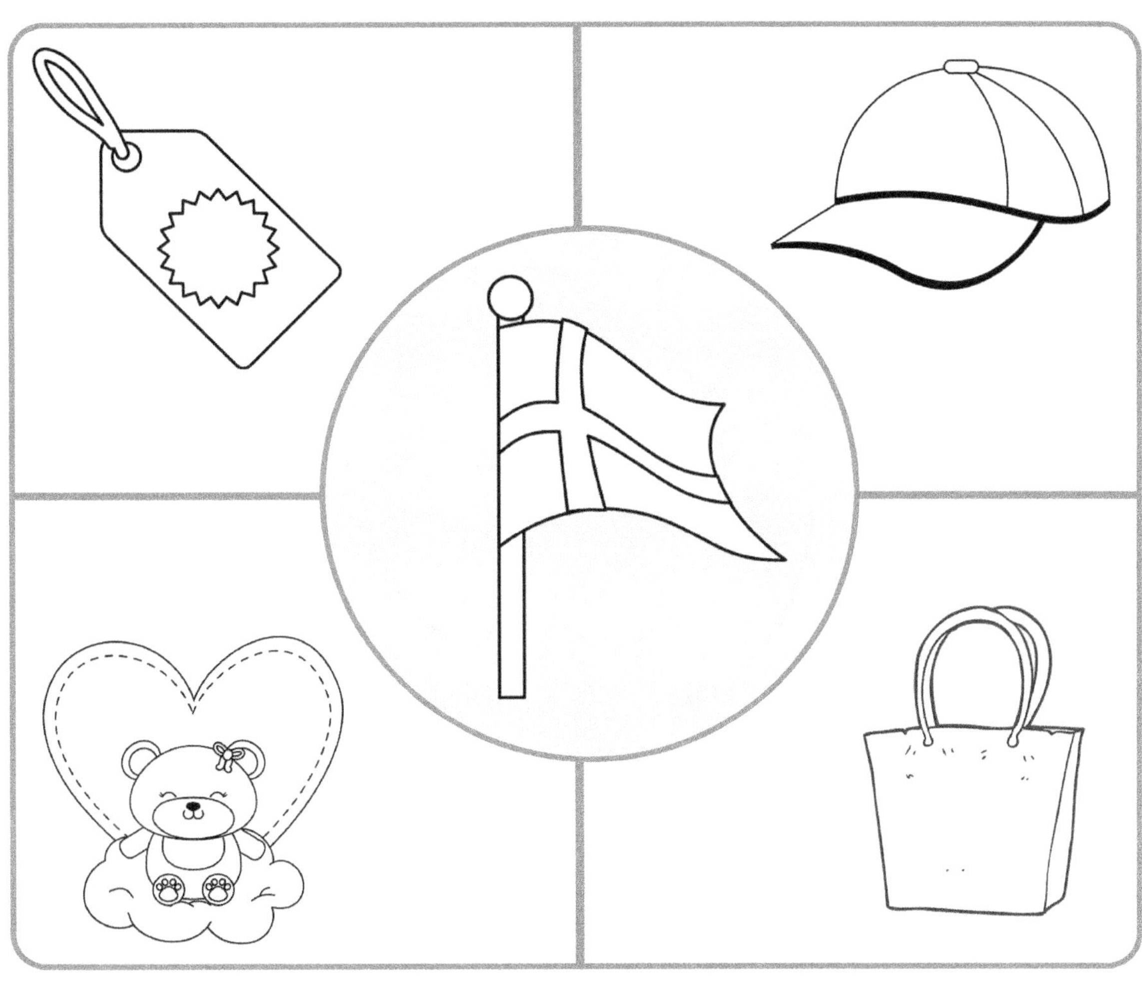

flag   tag   bag

Name:

Say the picture in the middle. Circle the pictures that rhymes with it. Trace the rhyming words below.

ball   mall   tall

ball   mall   tall

ball   mall   tall

Name:

Say the picture in the middle. Circle the pictures that rhymes with it. Trace the rhyming words below.

map   trap   nap

map   trap   nap

map   trap   nap

Name:

Say the picture in the middle. Circle the pictures that rhymes with it. Trace the rhyming words below.

tart

heart

dart

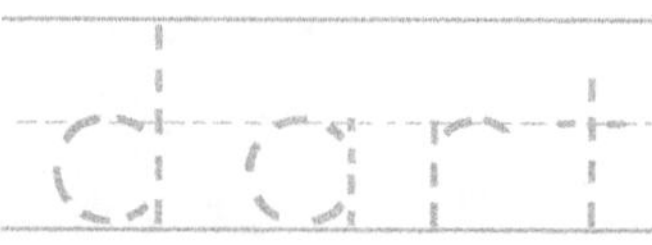

Name:

Say the picture in the middle. Circle the pictures that rhymes with it. Trace the rhyming words below.

cat   hat   fat

Name:

Say the picture in the middle. Circle the pictures that rhymes with it. Trace the rhyming words below.

skate   plate   gate

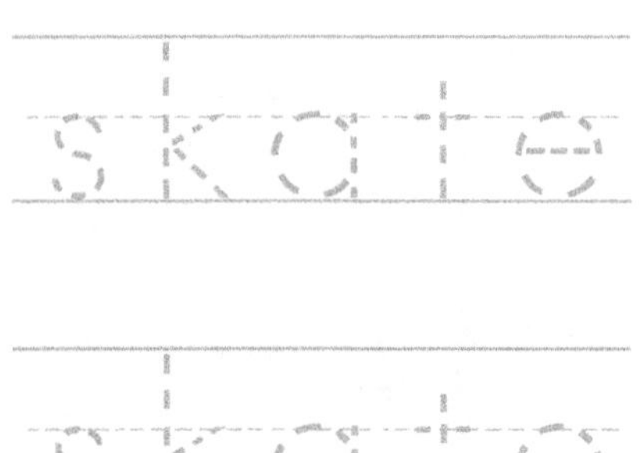

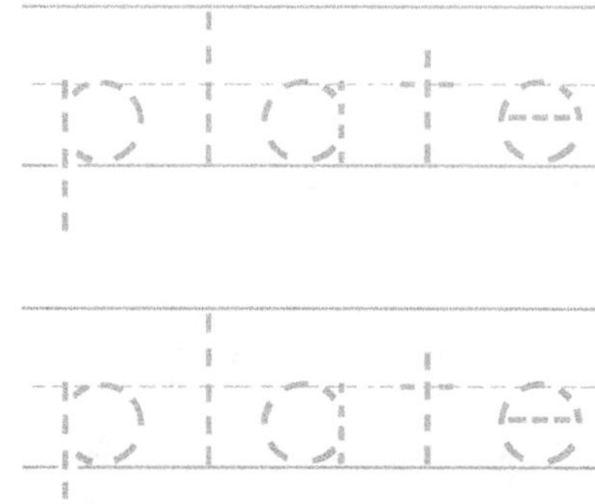

Name:

Say the picture in the middle. Circle the pictures that rhymes with it. Trace the rhyming words below.

three   tree   key

Name:

Say the picture in the middle. Circle the pictures that rhymes with it. Trace the rhyming words below.

sheep   jeep   sweep

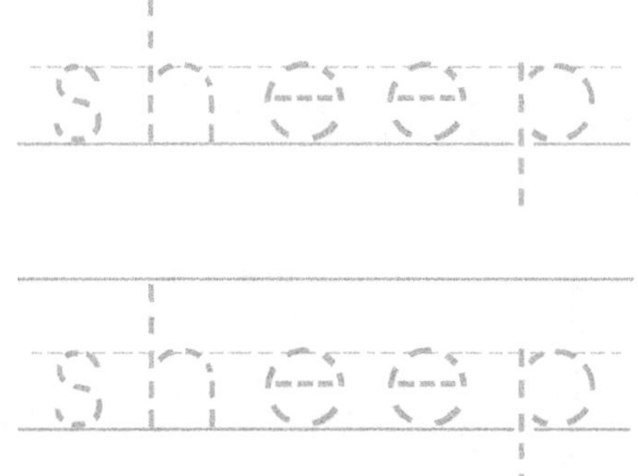

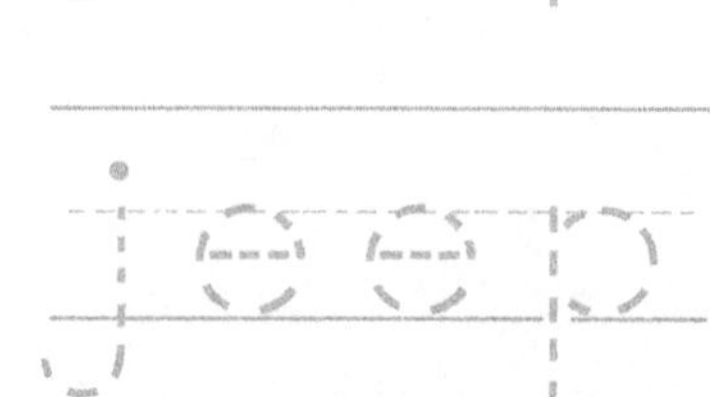

Name:

Say the picture in the middle. Circle the pictures
that rhymes with it. Trace the rhyming words below.

hen   ten   pen

Name:

Say the picture in the middle. Circle the pictures that rhymes with it. Trace the rhyming words below.

dig   pig   twig

Name:

Say the picture in the middle. Circle the pictures that rhymes with it. Trace the rhyming words below.

sit   kit   hit

Name:

Look at the picture. Color the word that rhymes.

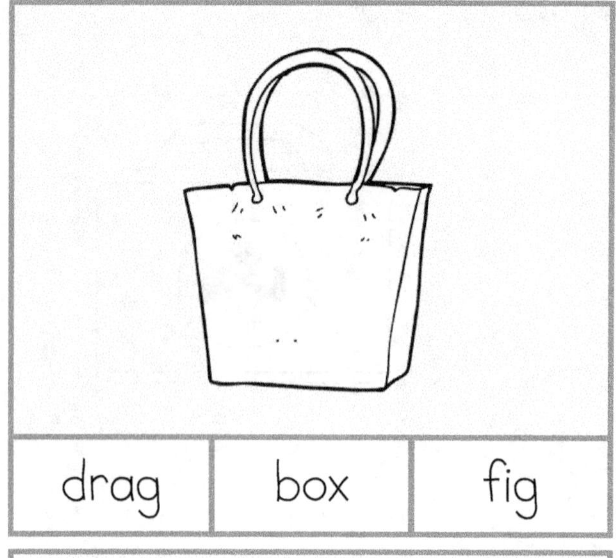

| drag | box | fig |

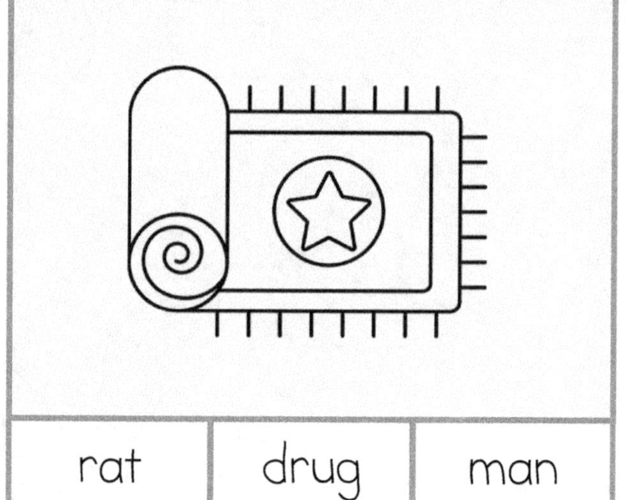

| rat | drug | man |

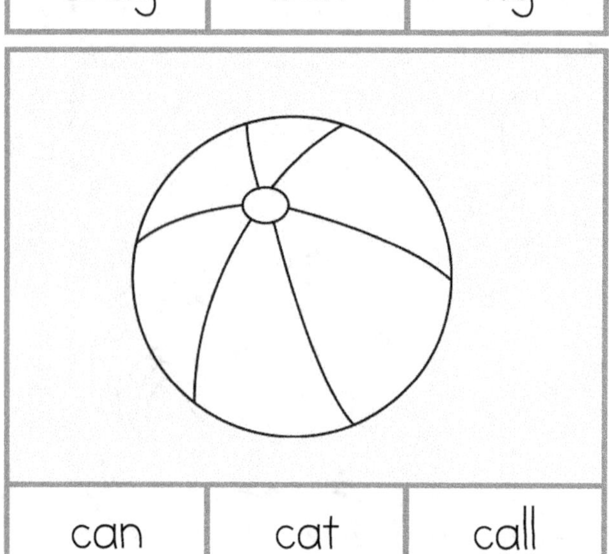

| can | cat | call |

| done | do | did |

| can | cap | cant |

| jug | june | jane |

Name:

Look at the picture. Color the word that rhymes.

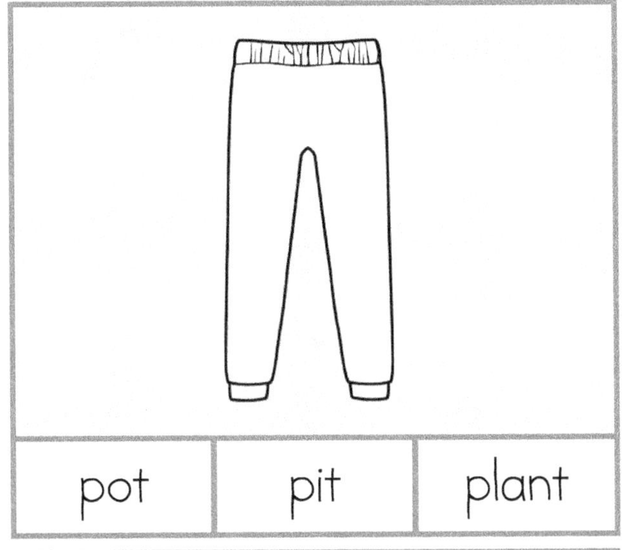

| pot | pit | plant |

| dell | dog | dig |

| hug | hunt | hide |

| wing | run | tag |

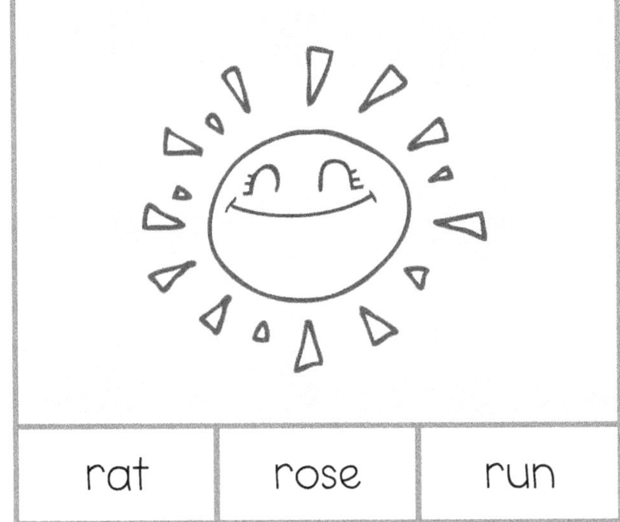

| rat | rose | run |

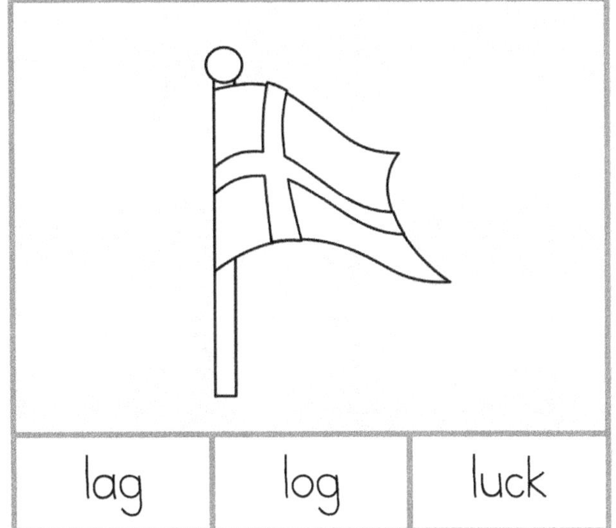

| lag | log | luck |

Name:

Look at the picture. Color the word that rhymes.

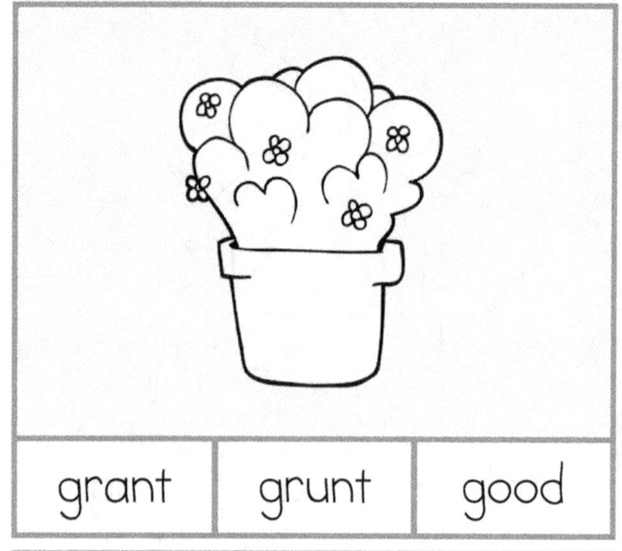

| grant | grunt | good |

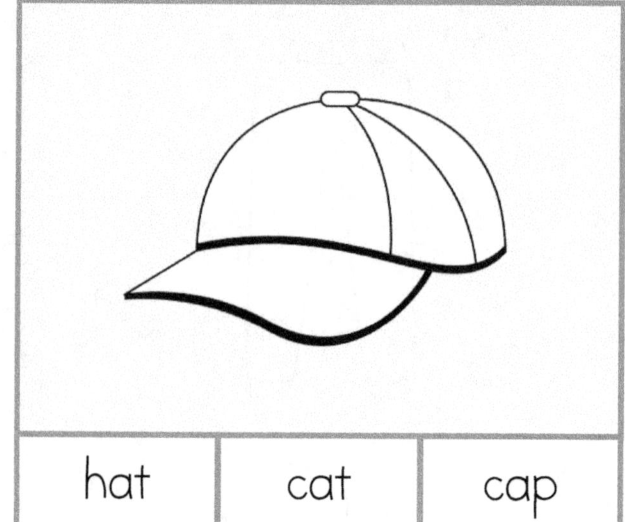

| hat | cat | cap |

| fin | fan | fun |

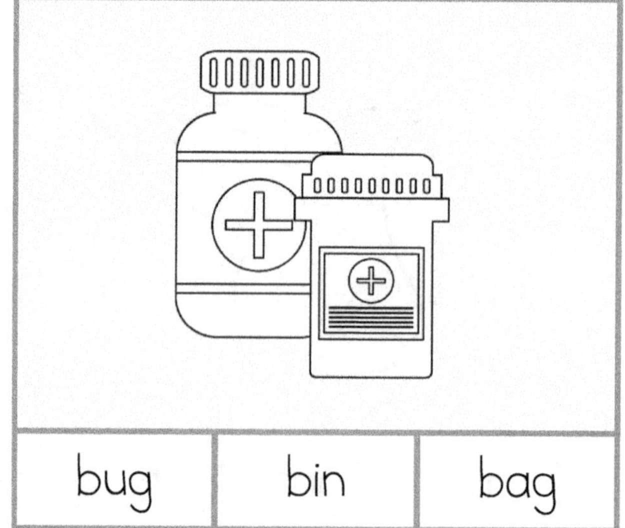

| bug | bin | bag |

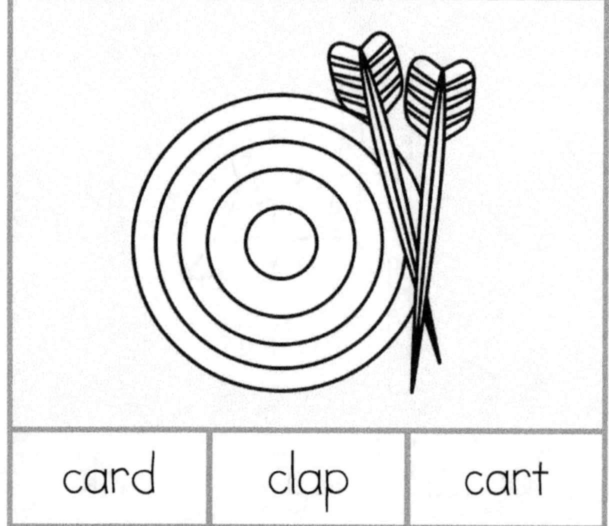

| card | clap | cart |

| pin | pan | pat |

Name:

Look at the picture. Color the word that rhymes.

| one | do | did |

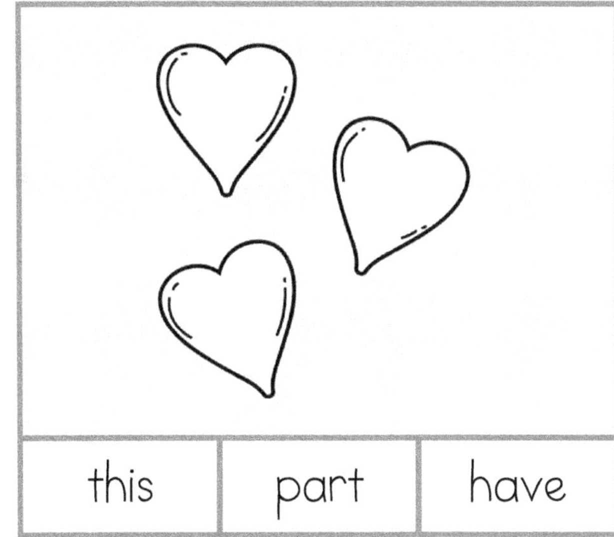

| this | part | have |

| that | this | they |

| down | buck | first |

| big | be | hub |

| home | help | plate |

Name:

Look at the picture. Color the word that rhymes.

| day | date | did |

| loud | love | like |

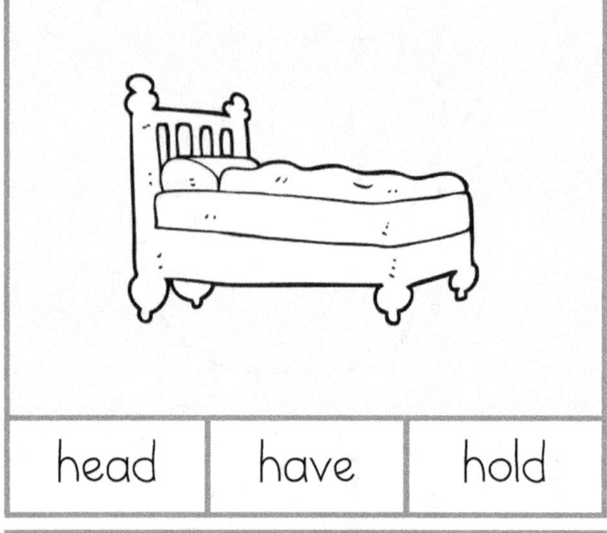

| head | have | hold |

| pink | red | blue |

| use | bed | can |

| it | in | we |

Name:

Look at the picture. Color the word that rhymes.

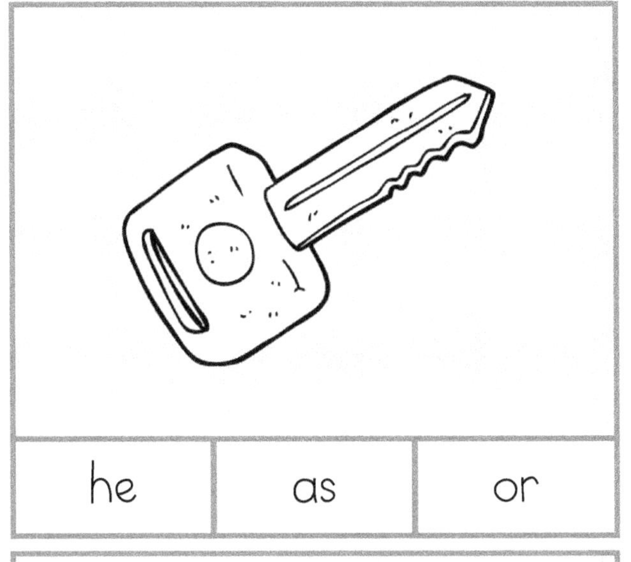

| he | as | or |

| and | pub | any |

| too | at | tug |

| jump | keep | some |

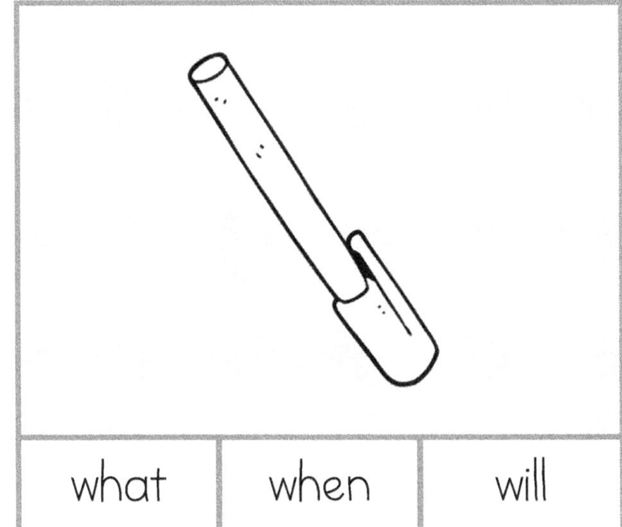

| what | when | will |

| much | not | box |

Name:

Look at the picture. Color the word that rhymes.

| leap | from | some |

| ten | one | day |

| she | out | key |

| drag | drag | drag |

| drag | drag | drag |

| drag | drag | drag |

Name:

Look at the picture. Color the word that rhymes.

| just | tuck | time |

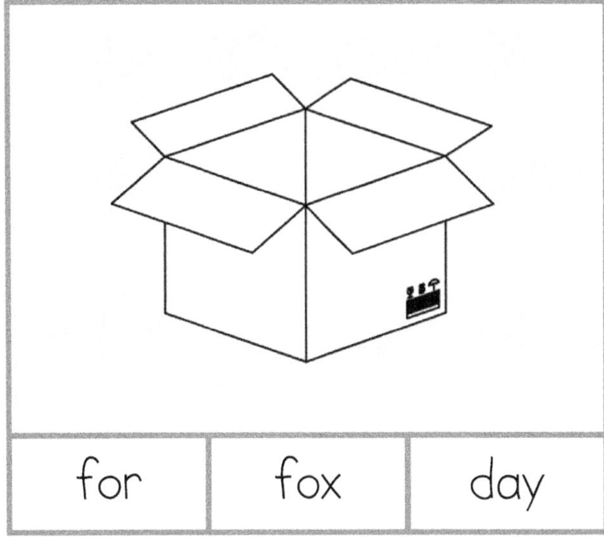

| for | fox | day |

| fish | frog | find |

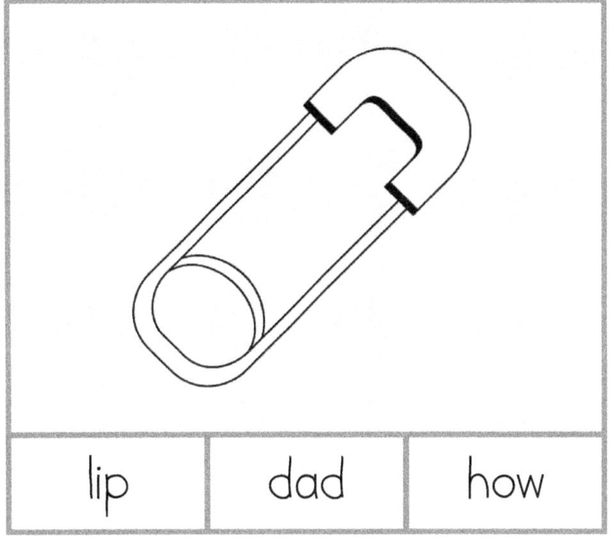

| lip | dad | how |

| give | his | big |

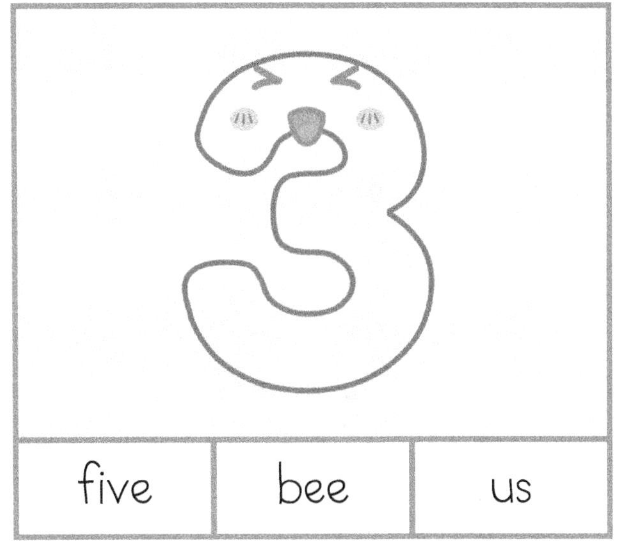

| five | bee | us |

Name:

Look at the picture. Color the word that rhymes.

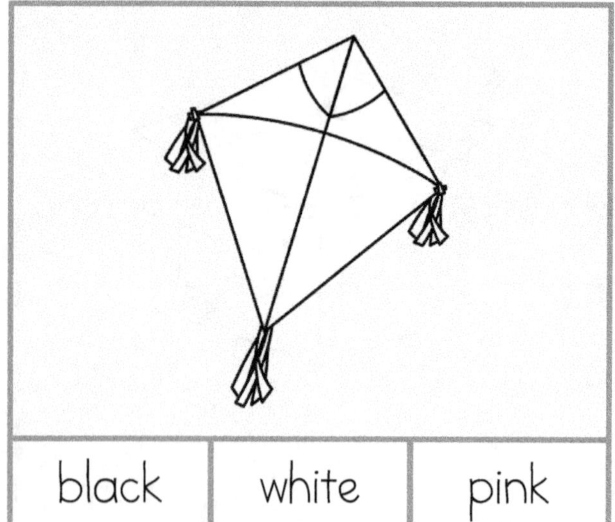

| black | white | pink |

| may | dog | hen |

| big | it | boy |

| been | said | dish |

| walk | this | jeep |

| jam | just | back |

Name:

Look at the picture. Color the word that rhymes.

goat	this	has

when	dock	have

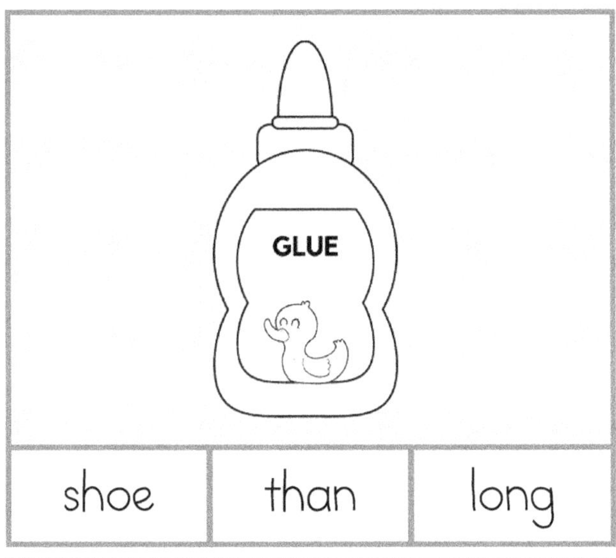

shoe	than	long

look	again	towel

each	house	said

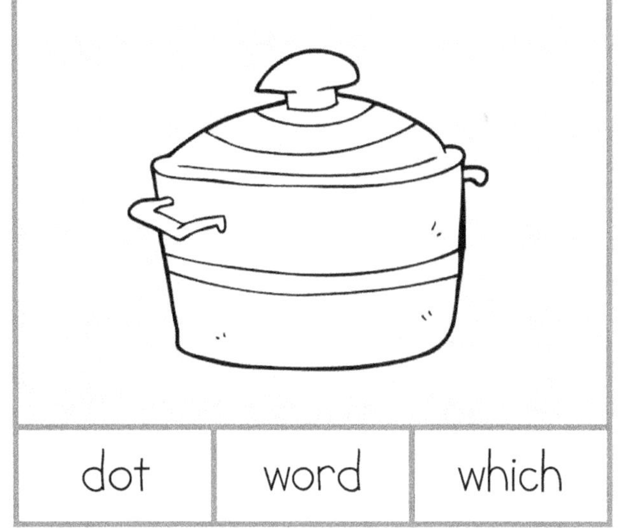

dot	word	which

Name:

Look at the picture. Color the word that rhymes.

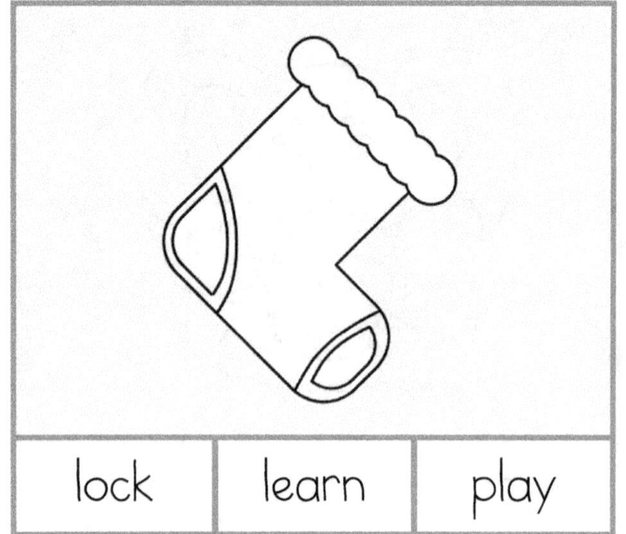

lock	learn	play

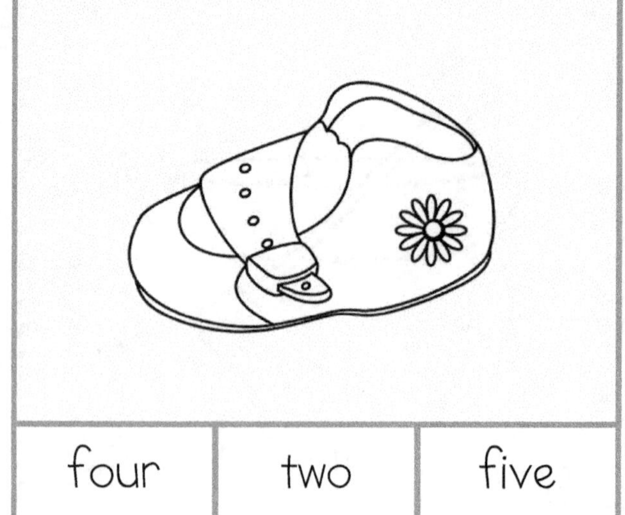

four	two	five

coat	come	bowl

all	was	log

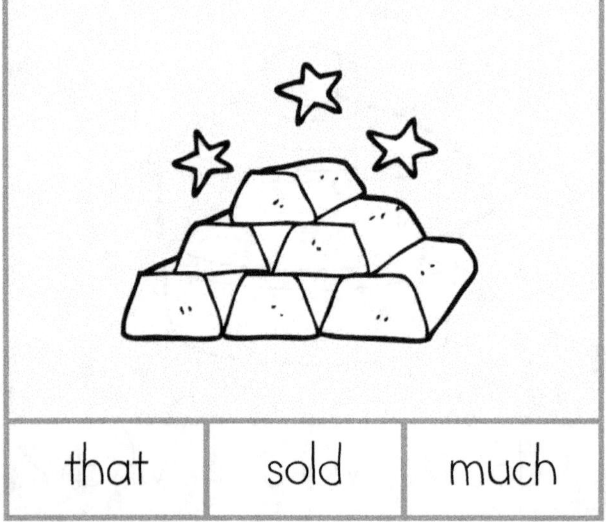

that	sold	much

cook	could	use

Name:

Look at the picture. Color the word that rhymes.

| about | hold | but |

| she | part | look |

| write | log | out |

| house | wood | boat |

| sat | zoo | sad |

| shall | should | shock |

Name: ____________________

Look at the picture. Color the word that rhymes.

| told | was | and |

| hog | not | we |

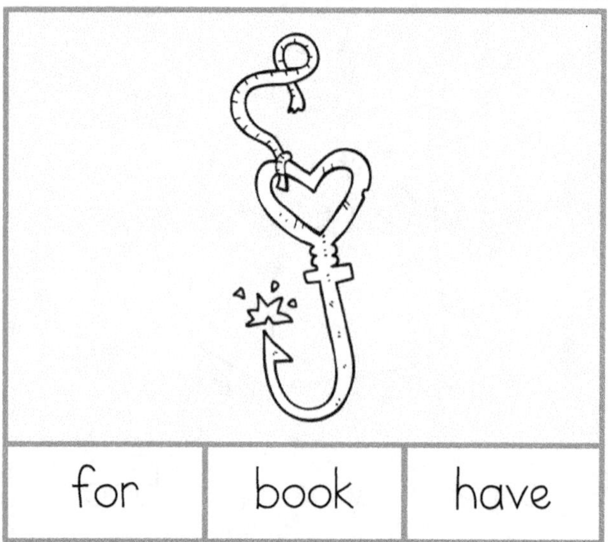

| for | book | have |

| back | some | spoon |

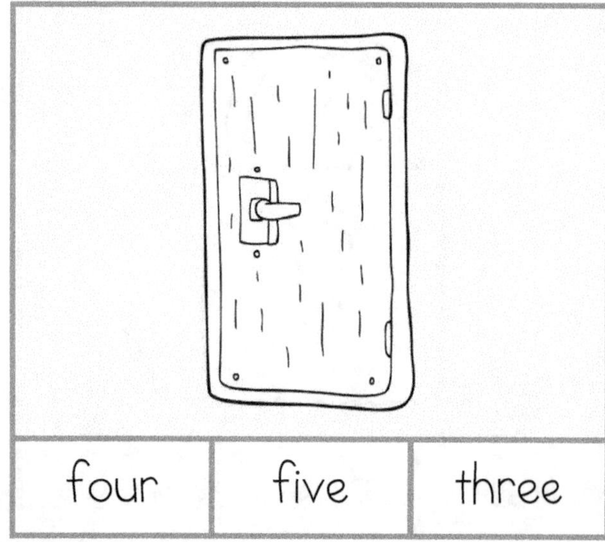

| four | five | three |

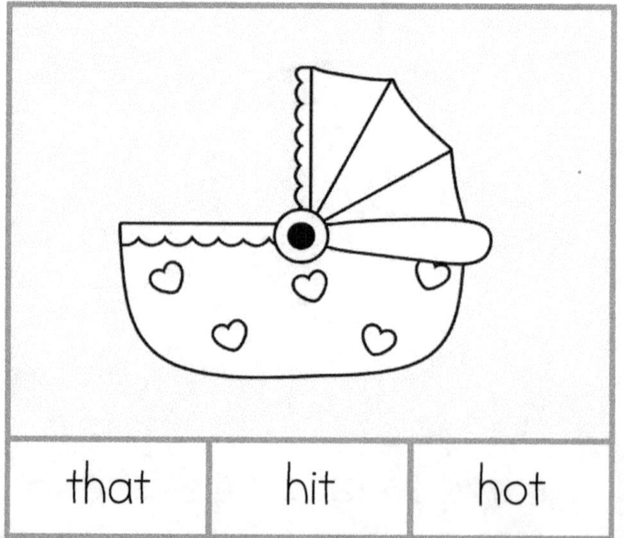

| that | hit | hot |

Name:

Look at the picture. Color the word that rhymes.

| may | noon | could |

| part | pour | pink |

| lot | will | out |

| they | mouse | out |

| been | like | vowel |

| hike | find | more |

RHYMING WORDS

Name:

Look at the picture. Color the word that rhymes.

| too | one | win |

| joy | with | can |

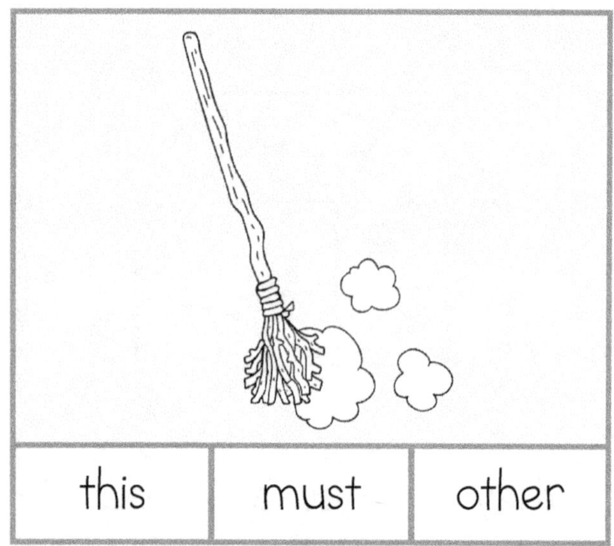

| this | must | other |

| me | plus | these |

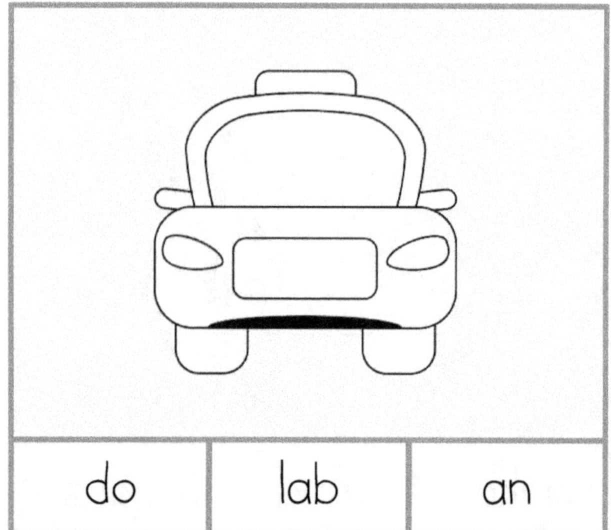

| do | lab | an |

| have | hand | lamb |

Name:

Look at the picture. Color the word that rhymes.

| grab | where | out |

| once | make | heard |

| bless | been | very |

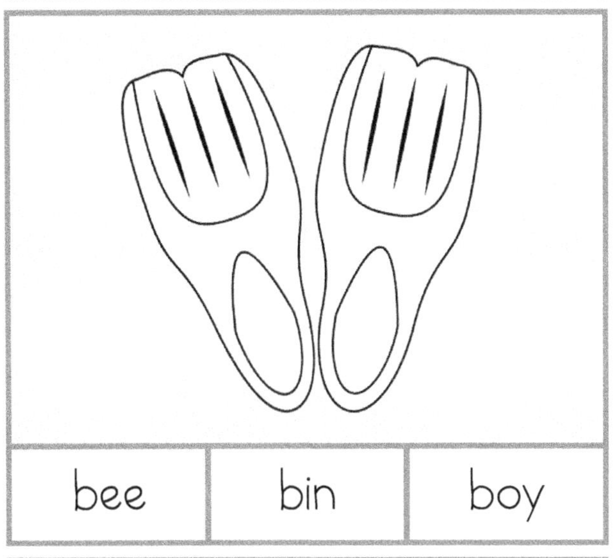

| bee | bin | boy |

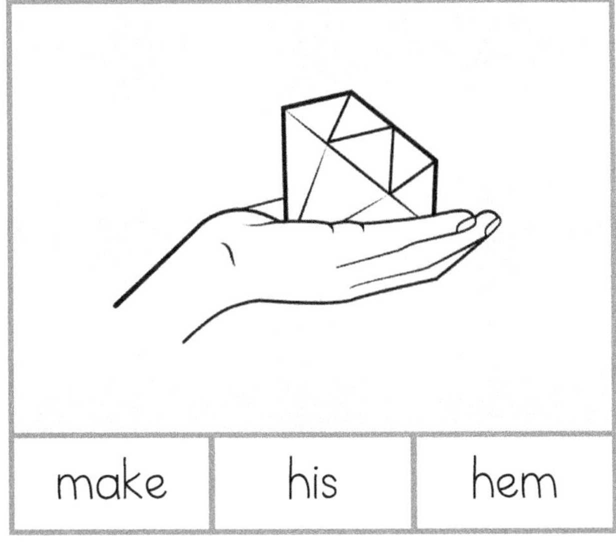

| make | his | hem |

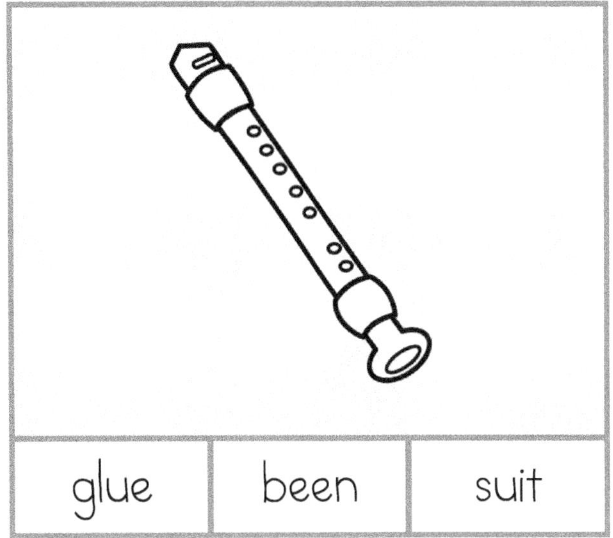

| glue | been | suit |

Name:

Look at the picture. Color the word that rhymes.

| dry | may | your |

| come | curl | walk |

| way | dove | think |

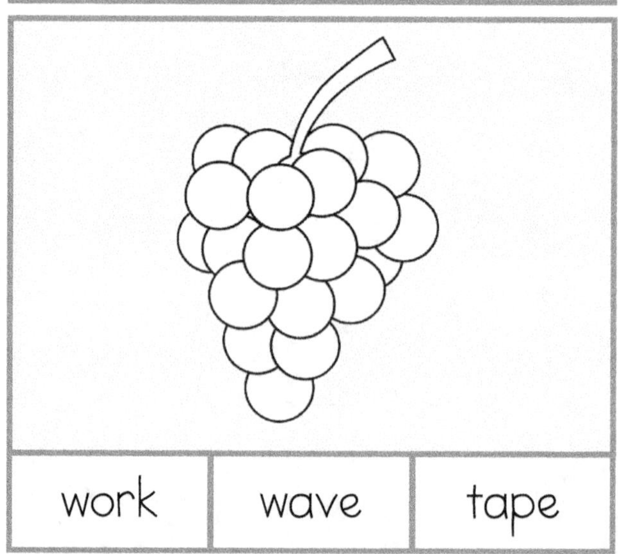

| work | wave | tape |

| hair | mom | long |

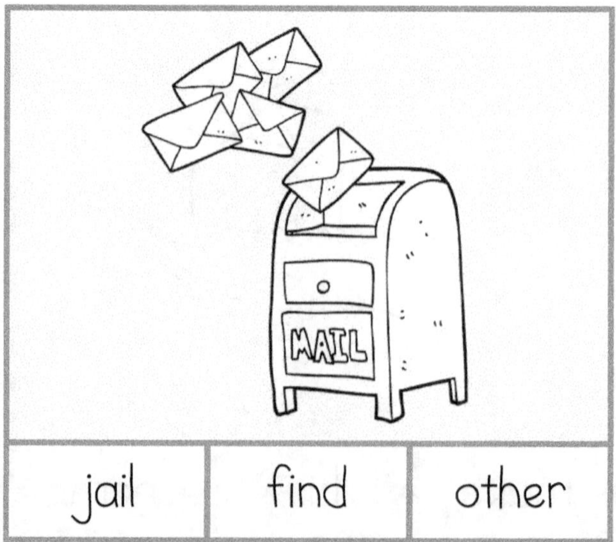

| jail | find | other |

Name:

Look at the picture. Color the word that rhymes.

| drag | hut | your |

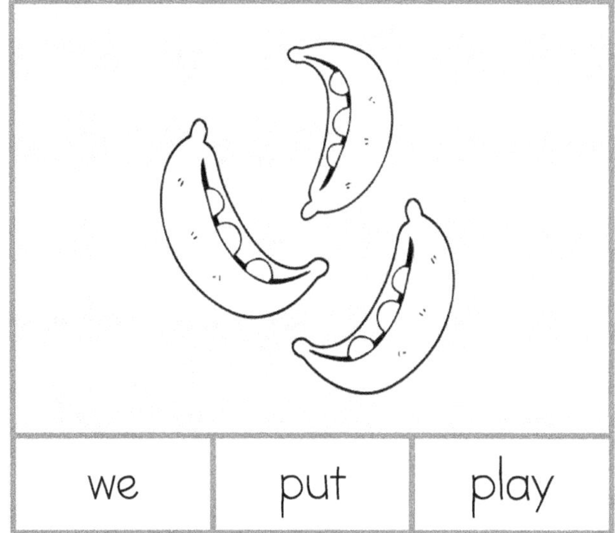

| we | put | play |

| more | nice | tin |

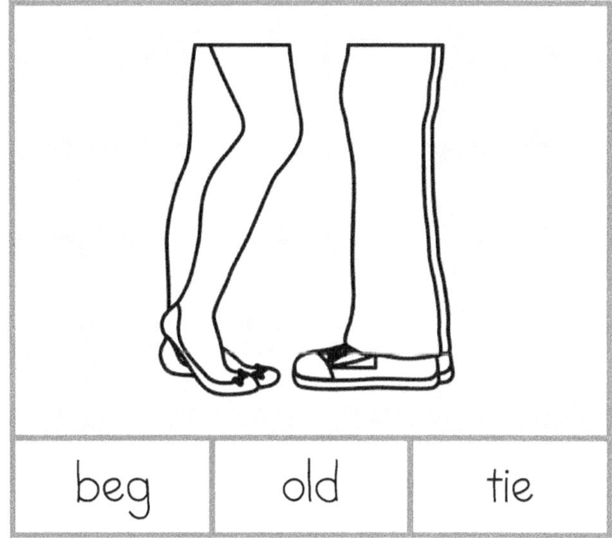

| beg | old | tie |

| bake | jump | just |

| high | been | went |

Name:

RHYMING WORDS

FUN RHYME

Read the words and color the pictures.

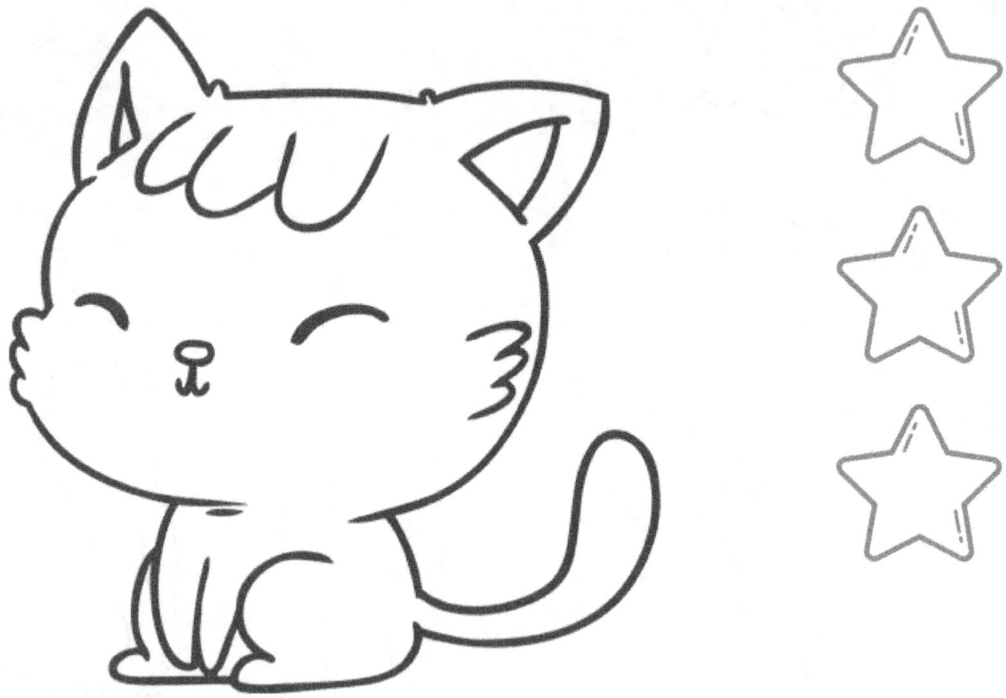

cat

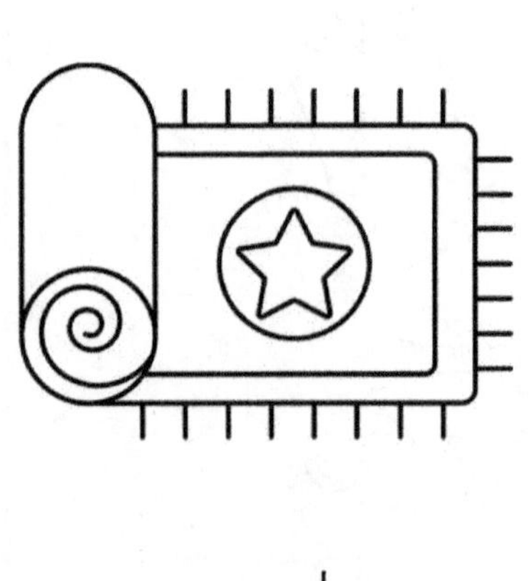

mat

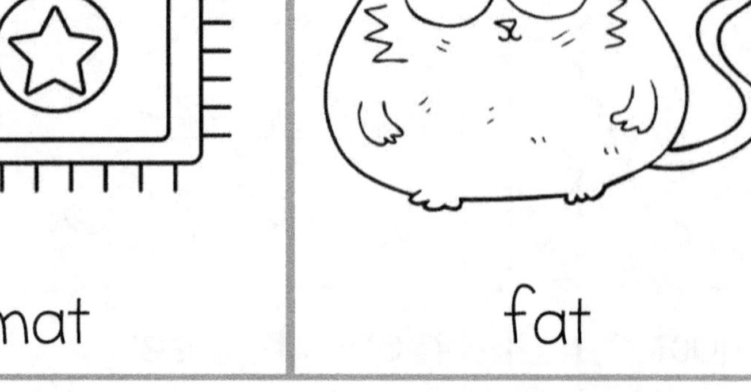

fat

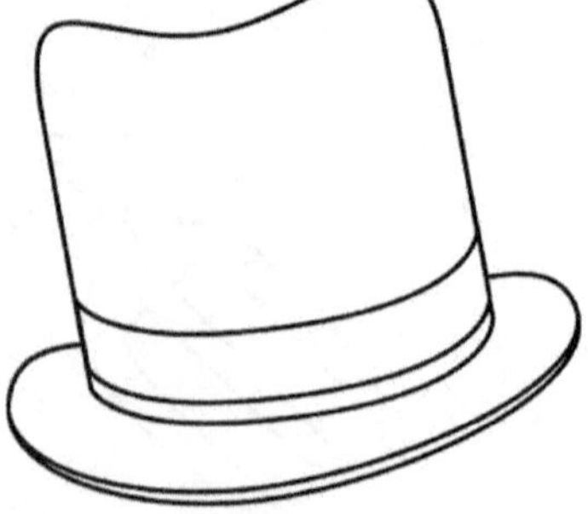

hat

Name:

FUN RHYME

Read the words and color the pictures.

tart

heart

dart

chart

Name:

FUN RHYME

Read the words and color the pictures.

skate

eight

gate

plate

Name:

RHYMING WORDS

FUN RHYME

Read the words and color the pictures.

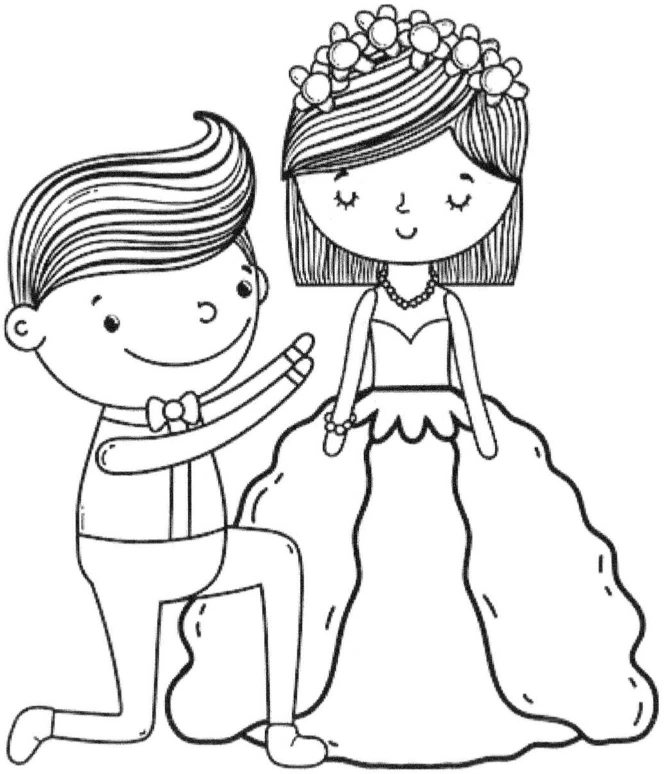

wed

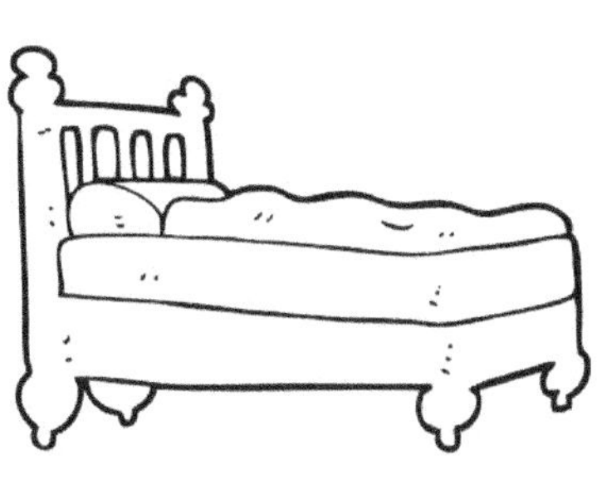

bed

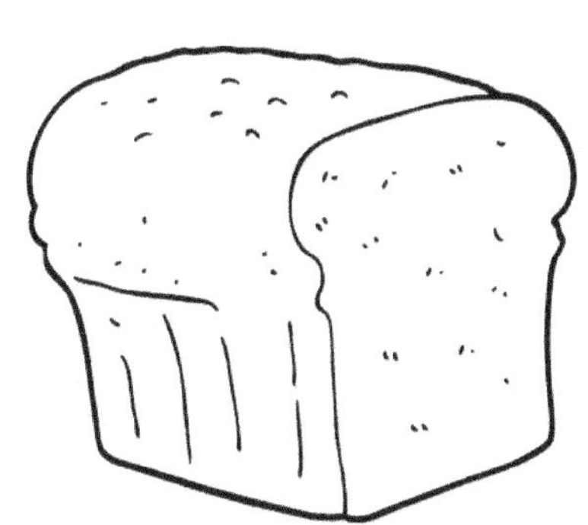

bread

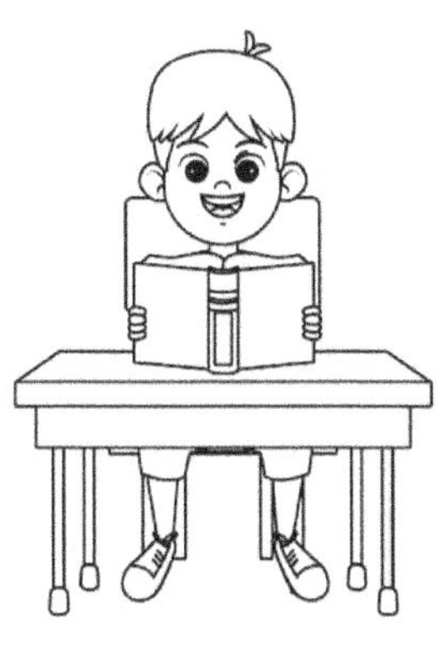

read

Name:

FUN RHYME

Read the words and color the pictures.

FUN RHYME

Read the words and color the pictures.

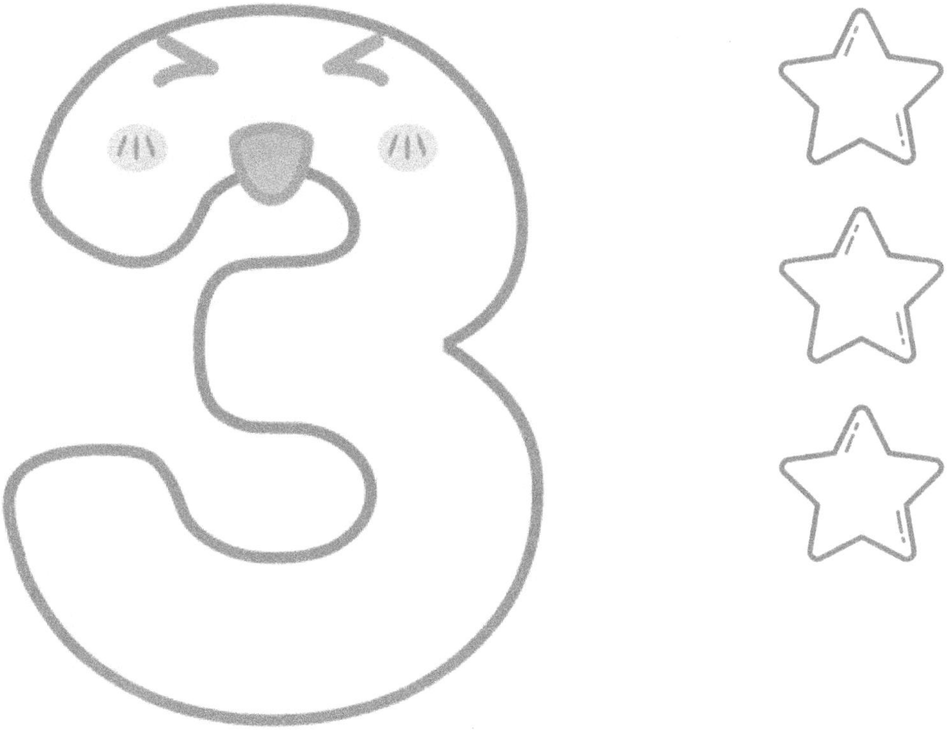

3

three

key

bee

tree

FUN RHYME

Read the words and color the pictures.

sheep

jeep

sleep

sweep

Name:

RHYMING WORDS

FUN RHYME

Read the words and color the pictures.

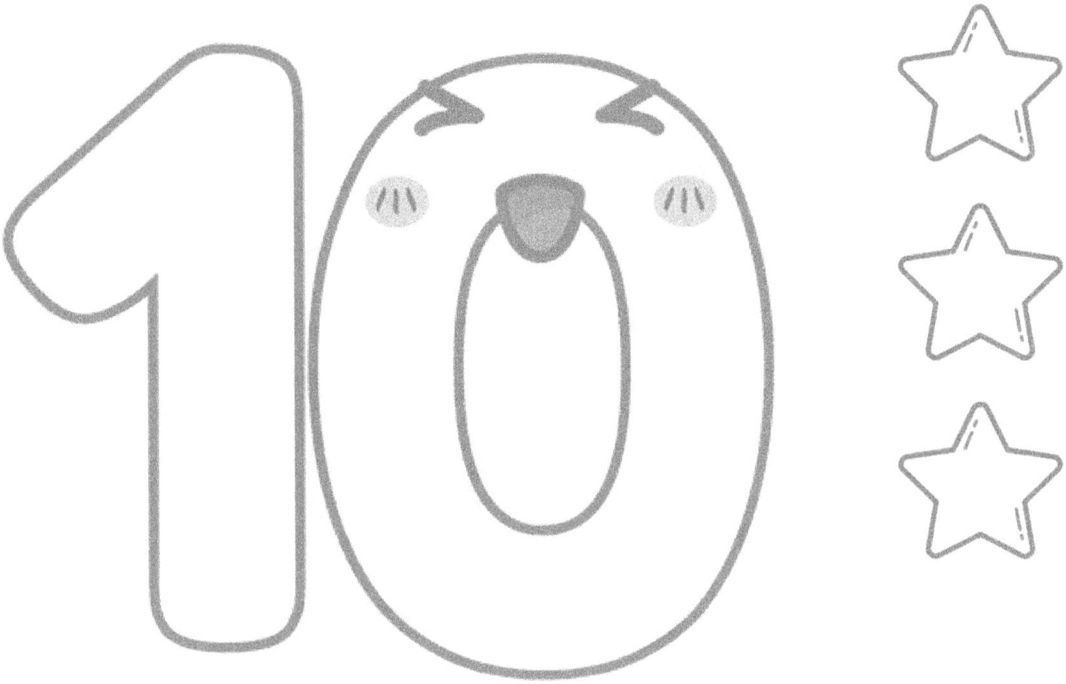

ten

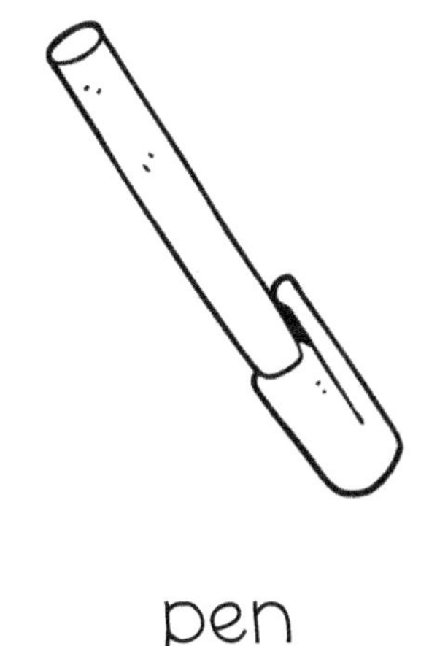

pen

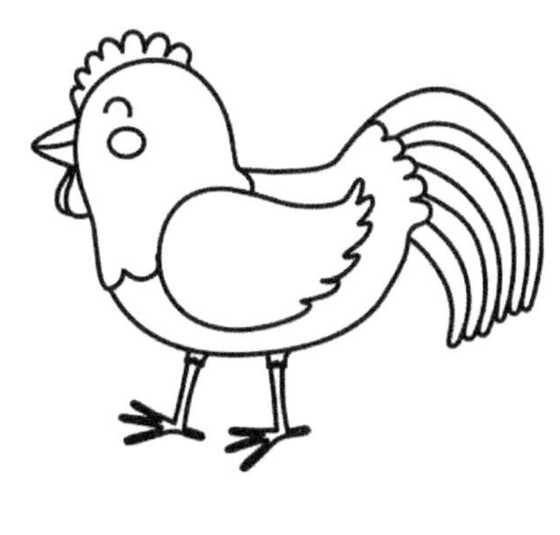

hen

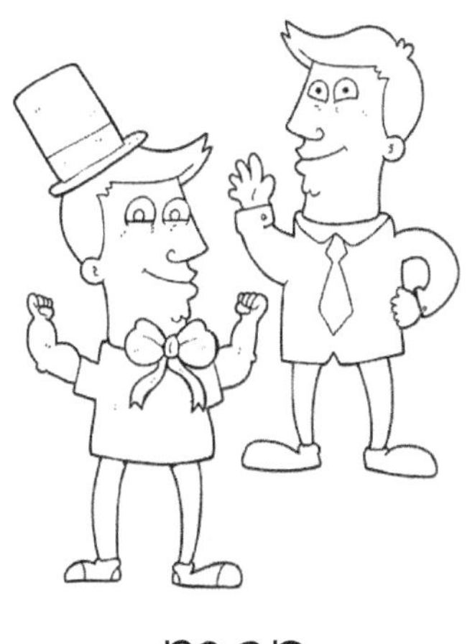

men

FUN RHYME

Read the words and color the pictures.

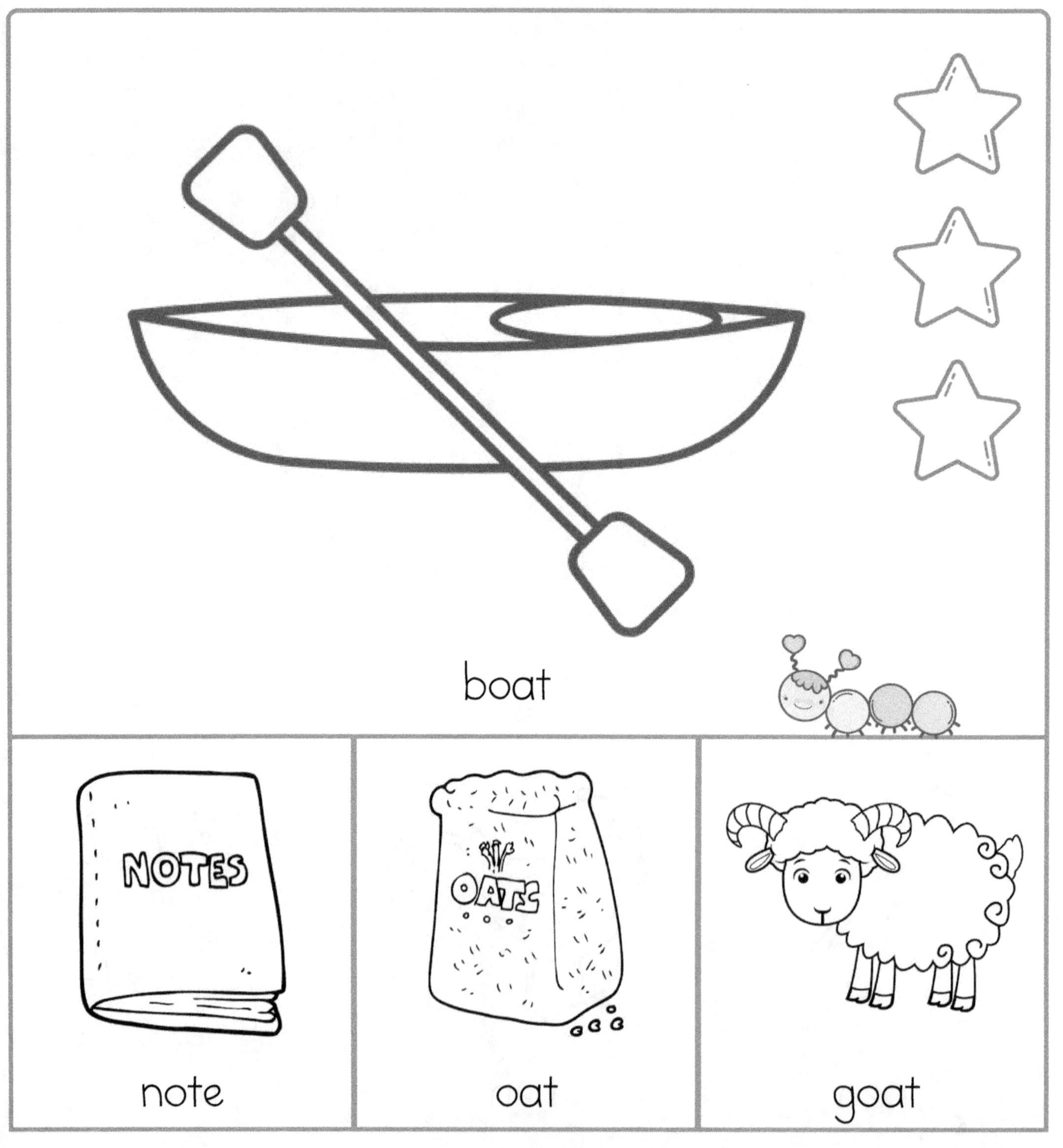

boat

note

oat

goat

FUN RHYME

Read the words and color the pictures.

jug

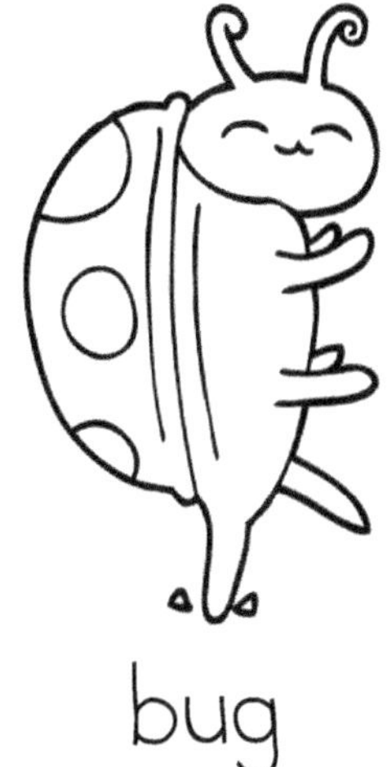

bug

mug

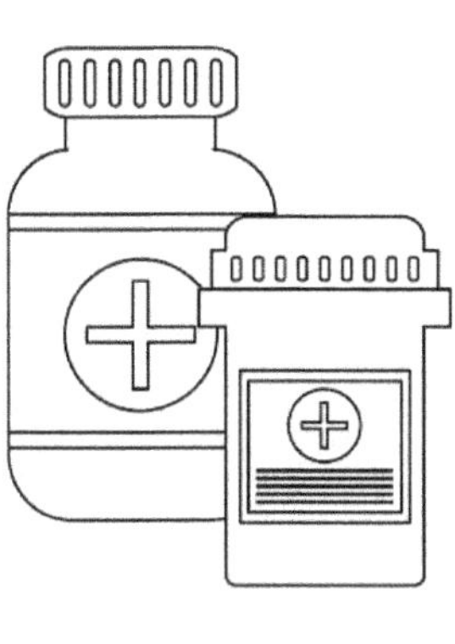

drug

Name:

FUN RHYME

Read the words and color the pictures.

run

sun

gun

one

Name:

Making new rhyming words.

Word	Rhyme with	Trace the word
hike		bike
fin		bin
plus		bus
joy		boy
map		cap

Name:

Making new rhyming words.

Word	Rhyme with	Trace the word
pen		hen
tube		cube
hug		rug
glad		dad
skirt		shirt

Name:

Making new rhyming words.

Word	Rhyme with	Trace the word
trap		clap
go		crow
jam		clam
tire		fire
boot		flute

Name: _______________

Making new rhyming words.

Word	Rhyme with	Trace the word
day		play
grab		grab
hot		cot
them		gem
why		cry

Name:

Making new rhyming words.

Word	Rhyme with	Trace the word
curl		girl
love		glove
who		glue
class		grass
fit		hit

Name:

Making new rhyming words.

Word	Rhyme with	Trace the word
group	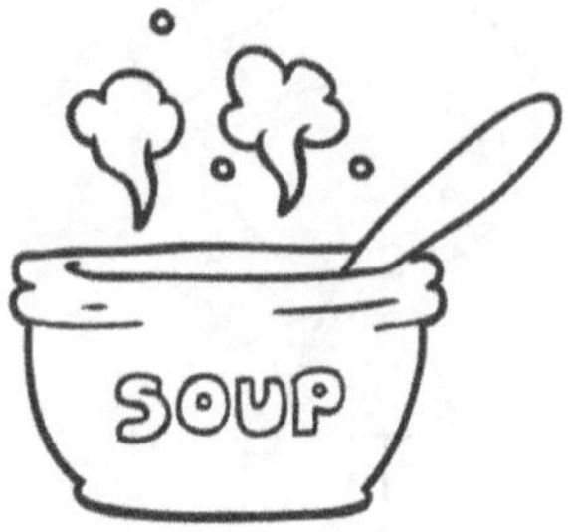 SOUP	soup
make	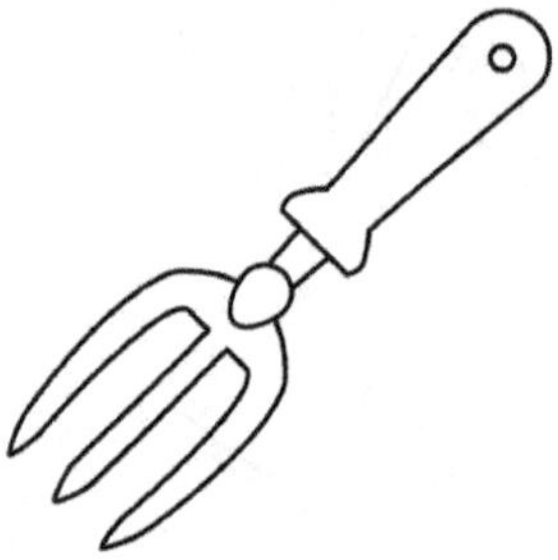	rake
lot	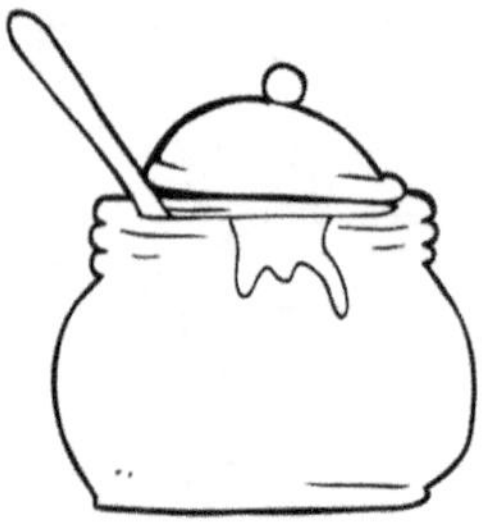	pot
ship	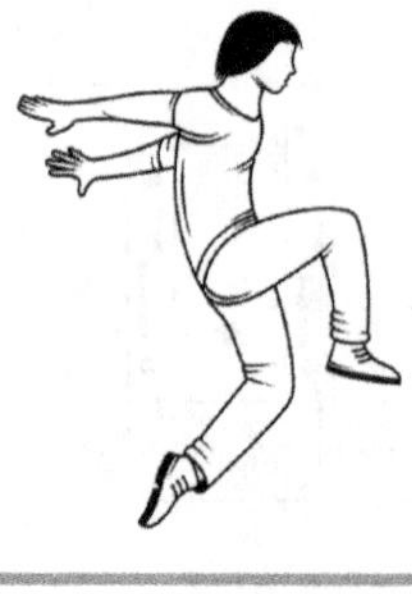	skip
when	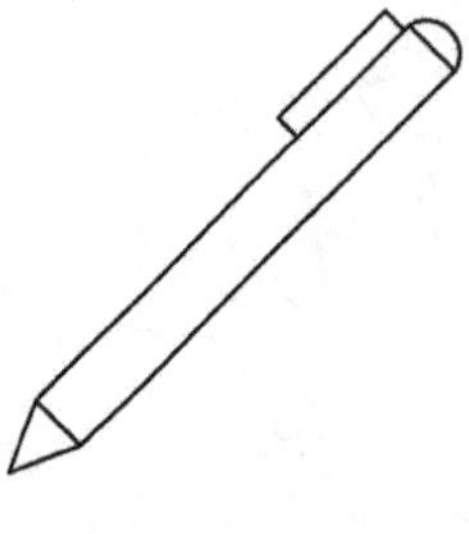	pen

Name:

Making new rhyming words.

Word	Rhyme with	Trace the word
knee		pea
hut		nut
must		dust
pet		jet
beef		leaf